THE VAUXHALL COMPANION

First model to be sold to the public, in 1903. Single-cylinder 5 hp engine mounted horizontally. Two forward speeds, no reverse. All-round coil-spring suspension, and tiller steering.

THE VAUXHALL COMPANION

Kenneth Ullyett

STANLEY PAUL / LONDON

STANLEY PAUL & CO. LTD

178–202 Great Portland Street, London W1

AN IMPRINT OF THE  HUTCHINSON GROUP

London Melbourne Sydney
Auckland Johannesburg Cape Town
and agencies throughout the world

First published 1971

ACKNOWLEDGEMENTS

It is a matter of solid fact that Vauxhall, once the builders of such internationally famed sporting cars as the 20 hp, the Prince Henry and the 30/98—cars which made British motoring and motor sport illustrious in the first generation of automobilism—has been since 1925 an integral part of General Motors Corporation, the world's largest producers of vehicles by far. It is surely a reasonable viewpoint that Vauxhall benefits from the best of both worlds, having a tradition of craftsmanship allied to the largest capital resources and the best-equipped car-engineering research centres in the world.

In the United Kingdom Vauxhall Motors Limited produce a range of cars including many variants of the Viva, Victor, Ventora, Cresta and Viscount, and these have a devoted following, while in the ranks of the Vintage Sports Car Club, and of other clubs specialising in vintage Vauxhalls, there are devotees of the 30/98, the 23/60, the R-type and many other great cars of former years. It is a fascinating story ranging over nearly 70 years, from the days when the Vauxhall Iron Works built only about 40 cars in an entire year, to the present era when some 146,000 cars are built each year for home sales, and nearly as many for export. One in every six cars on the roads of Britain now is a Vauxhall, and the men and women building these cars at Luton and Ellesmere Port (coupled with Bedford trucks, bus and coach chassis built at Dunstable) have a total payroll including holiday pay of some £47·5 million. The total value of exports is usually something like £82 million annually, and, of course, this is all to the benefit of the nation.

The Vauxhall story tells how a small marine-engineering works in Vauxhall Walk, in Thames-side London, has grown to become a highly organised industrial undertaking, employing many skills of a large number of people.

This book is the author's personal account of the Vauxhall organisation. Although the Company provided much reference and factual material, the thoughts and opinions expressed are those of the author.

In *The Vauxhall Companion*, eighth in the Stanley Paul series of *Companion* books, I have endeavoured to cover all aspects of the long Vauxhall records. In this I have been given most ready help by many sections of Vauxhall Motors at the various production centres, and by a number of people inside the Company and out who have contributed material, or given permission for reproduction of historic photographs and records. They include the editors of *Autocar* and *Automobile Engineer*, Captain W. J. Bentley, W. Boddy and *Motor Sport* (without whose accurate records it is difficult for any book to be written if it deals with motor-sporting events of the past), Dudley Coram, L. C. Darbyshire, Glyn Davies, Ron Evans (supervisor, factory visits at Luton and Dunstable plants), Edward Eves, Bill Farbon, E. W. Hancock, O.B.E., M.I.Mech.E., F.R.S.A., Eyre & Spottiswoode Ltd., Derek Goatman (Vauxhall's Chief Press Officer), T. W. Holtom, Gwyn Hughes (Vauxhall Motors Publications Editor), Percy C. Kidner, Michael Marr (Public Relations Manager, Vauxhall Motors), *Motor*, Motor Racing Publications Ltd., Maurice Platt, M.Eng., Laurence R. Pomeroy, Harry Pratt, George Sanders, Graham Turner (*The Car Makers*), Leslie Walton, and Kenneth Wickham, A.M.I.Mech.E.

KENNETH ULLYETT

THE ROYAL AUTOMOBILE CLUB
London

CONTENTS

ILLUSTRATIONS

The first model to be sold to the public *frontispiece*

Assembling a GM chassis in Detroit, 1922
The first Hydra-Matic transmission system
The Viva remote-control mechanism

Between pages 120 *and* 121
The prototype two-seater XVR
Twin 150 CD carburetters
Victor 2000
The Victor engine
Vauxhall's Styling Director, David Jones
GM's vice-president of styling, William L. Mitchell
Some of the world's richest and most powerful men
Vauxhall's $13\frac{1}{2}$-acre Engineering Centre at Luton

I

Royal Gardens

'Let us then step into the coach, and be off to the Gardens', wrote William Makepeace Thackeray, recounting the romance of Miss Becky Sharp in *Vanity Fair* in the early 1800's.

These Royal Gardens to which in rich imagination Thackeray takes us, along with Becky, Dobbin, Jos, Rawdon and the other characters in his *chef-d'œuvre*, are the Vauxhall Gardens, which within that same nineteenth century were to give their name to the first Vauxhall engineering works.

London then was rich in pleasure gardens, Ranelagh, Cremorne and others vying with Vauxhall to attract young lovers and pickpockets, gamesters and rogues. And as to what Vauxhall was really like around 1833 (the end of the period of *Vanity Fair*, which was published in 1847), Thackeray summed it up in one graphic, descriptive sentence:

'. . . of all the delights of the Gardens; of the hundred thousand *extra* lamps, which were always lighted; the fiddlers in cocked hats, who played ravishing melodies under the gilded cockle-shell in the midst of the Gardens; the singers, both of comic and sentimental ballads, who charmed ears there; the country dances, formed by bouncing cockneys and cockneyesses, and executed amidst jumping, thumping, and laughter; the signal which announced that Madame Saqui was about to mount skywards on a slack-rope ascending to the stars; the hermit that always sat in the illuminated hermitage; the dark walks, so favourable to the interviews of young lovers; the pots of stout handed about by the people in the shabby old liveries;

and the twinkling boxes, in which the happy feasters make-believe to eat slices of almost invisible ham . . .'

The crest over the archway leading into the 'Royal' Gardens (this title was honorary, since gossips said George IV—'The First Gentleman'—desported himself there) had a crest displayed above, incorporating the symbol of the griffin. According to the Royal College of Heralds, the griffin is a mythical creature, half eagle and half lion, the sort of animal which appeared so often on early English heraldic devices. One need not be in doubt as to what the heraldic artists believed it looked like, for it is to be seen today on every Vauxhall car and on most major pieces of literature and stationery concerned with Vauxhall Motors Limited, whose headquarters is at Luton, Bedfordshire.

A most curious coincidence had made this possible, for the Vauxhall's griffin crest came from Luton in the first place, the original holder of this heraldic device being a medieval desperado and soldier of fortune serving at the court of King John. This pioneer of the griffin, Fulk le Breant, was awarded the Manor of Luton for his services to the King, and by royal command married Margaret de Redvers, widow of Baldwin de Redvers, son of the Earl of Devon. By that marriage Fulk acquired her fortune, including her house at Lambeth near the Thames. Fulk and his bride occupied this house when in London, and the property soon became known as Fulk's Hall, later gradually corrupted to Fawkes Hall, and thus in Norman-French manner to Vauxhall.

Fulk le Breant's fortunes changed on the death of King John in 1216, and he was exiled to France, where it is said he died in poverty. Nothing is known of Fulk's Hall for over 400 years until in the year 1661 the estate was opened to the public as a pleasure garden. The diarist Evelyn mentions visiting the 'New Spring Gardens', as it was first called shortly after the opening.

The area later to become the birthplace of the Vauxhall car was originally simply a garden, but Samuel Morland constructed a central music-and-gaming-room there in 1667, and this attracted many notable court personalities of the era of King Charles II and Nell Gwyn. Samuel Pepys mentions the Gardens in a number of Diary entries, referring to the charm of the natural setting, and the song of the nightingale: 'And here fiddlers, and there a harp, and here a Jew's trump, and here laughing, and there fine people walking.'

Later historians were fascinated by Vauxhall, since 'Spring Gardens' was the longest lived of all these places of pleasure and, when it closed, the oldest in London. Sir Walter Besant in his classic *London in the Eighteenth Century* (A. & C. Black) says: 'There were Bermondsey Spa and Lambeth Wells. All these spas became, first, places of public resort and amusement, then tea-gardens, then taverns, then disreputable places . . . There were places which pretended to be nothing but gardens of pleasure . . . Foremost among them were Cuper's Gardens, the gardens of Vauxhall, of Ranelagh, of Marylebone, and the notorious Temples of Flora and Apollo . . . A short walk led the citizen who resided in Cheapside to the White Conduit House; a boat took him easily to Vauxhall . . . Here he could pass a pleasant evening with his wife and daughters: there were music and singing; there was dancing; there were performances on the tight-rope; there were fireworks; there was supper with port wine or punch. In these gardens all classes met freely; provided people behaved quietly it mattered nothing what their reputation might be; the worthy citizen and his daughters enjoyed their evening none the less because in the next alcove two or three rather noisy young gentlemen were entertaining two or three very joyous young ladies. Nor did it diminish their happiness to know that a notorious highway robber was parading the walks . . .' All this, and more, in much the same vein as *Vanity Fair*, but fact, not fiction.

In the early eighteenth century when Vauxhall was still known as Spring Gardens, the politician and literary celebrity Joseph Addison—pioneer of *The Tatler* and co-founder of

The Spectator—wrote of an evening when he went down the Thames to the Royal Gardens with Sir Roger de Coverley, whose name has been perpetuated in Olde Tyme dancing nowadays. Sir Walter Besant's records of Vauxhall tell that in 1733 the place was taken over by an impresario, Jonathan Tyer, on a twenty years' lease at £250 a year (probably the equivalent of £10,000 annually in this century) and that on the June opening night under his management there was a company of 400, including Frederick, Prince of Wales. Vauxhall remained in the hands of the Tyer family for 90 years, was eventually sold for £20,000, and finally closed in 1859. Besant's contemporary account written within half a century of Vauxhall's day, says that the Gardens: '. . . consisted of a quadrangular grove thickly planted with trees; four principal walks ran through them, crossed by others; there were clearances, so to speak, where were raised colonnades, alcoves, theatres, temples, an orchestra and a place for dancing....' And the Rt. Hon. George Canning, poet and orator who became Prime Minister in 1827, wrote of Vauxhall:

'Then oft returning from the green retreats
Where fair Vauxhallia decks her sylvan seats,
Where each spruce nymph from City counter free,
Sips the frothed syllabub or fragrant tea;
While with cliced ham, scraped beef and burnt champagne
Her 'prentice lover soothes his amorous pain.'

All these places, as Besant said, degenerated in turn to: 'tea-gardens, then taverns, and then disreputable places', and with the human race's well-known facility for destroying so much of what it touches, Vauxhall became industrialised and semi-derelict after 1859, when a concern known as Bish, Gye and Hughes finally found the pleasure gardens unprofitable. The coming of the railroad enabled working people to travel further, as did the horse-drawn shillibeers and omnibuses, and anyway the coming of Vauxhall Junction railway station destroyed any aesthetic appeal of Lambeth, Vauxhall and the nearby Thames-side areas.

All the same, it was the proximity of the Junction and the river which in 1857 attracted to London a Scottish marine engineer, Alexander Wilson. Little is known of his early life. Indeed, the only records of the first years of Vauxhall comes from the L. C. Darbyshire monograph detailed in the preface to this volume, aided by the memory of the late T. W. Holtom, who served with Vauxhall from 1888 to 1938, and of Mr. Leslie Walton, a director of the Company as long ago as 1907. Today historians have few other avenues for research, with one notable exception, and the following account of Vauxhall's early days leans entirely on the long-term research of L. C. Darbyshire.

Because of the past history of the Thames-side area, the small business founded by Alexander Wilson for building marine engines was known as the Vauxhall Iron Works. The first main office was in the Wandsworth Road (named after the River Wandle, which today is conduited and runs under London streets), a few minutes from Vauxhall Junction and the now forgotten Royal Gardens.

Wilson's business was successful, and he managed to secure British Admiralty contracts for the supply of high-pressure engines for pinnaces, and compound and triple-expansion engines for river tugs. Wilson provided the marine engines for many side-paddle and stern-wheeler ships, at least two of which were extremely popular with the London public until recent years. These were for the upriver pleasure steamers launched in the '90's, the *Queen Elizabeth* and *Cardinal Wolsey*, plying between Westminster Bridge and Hampton Court. It might indeed be said these ships were powered by the first ever Vauxhall engines of note: steam, of course. Additionally, from the Vauxhall Iron Works came donkey engines for boiler water-feed, the Excelsior steam-driven pump, and the Lightfoot dry-air refrigeration plant used for large-scale cold storage.

Like Royce and other great engineers of the past, Alexander Wilson was a practical engineer, not a man for account books, and in later years of Vauxhall this was to lead to financial difficulties and the appointment of an Official Receiver. Wilson's desk, according to one of his old employees, was usually covered by a mass of papers which nobody dared tidy nor disturb. Old envelopes and the backs of letters were used for making notes and rough engineering drawings, and were then stuffed into Wilson's pockets for future reference. At first this did not matter, since although his Company grew to employ some 150 men, it was very much a one-man band. So, too, was that of F. H. Royce & Co., Manchester, despite the loan of £50 by Royce's partner Claremont to help pay the firm's wages.

While Royce was concentrating on electricity, Wilson and the Vauxhall Iron Works dealt with steam—not only steam-powered marine engines, but boilers, shafting, propellers, donkey engines and auxiliaries. Vauxhall became a limited-liability company (corporation) in 1892, the financial pressure and expansion potential resulting in a marine consulting engineer Mr. W. Gardner taking the position of Managing Director, while Alexander Wilson remained on the board for a further two years.

In 1894 Wilson left to set up as a consulting engineer in Fenchurch Street, London. He was probably the last man to realise it, but he had created at Vauxhall the sort of plant which could manufacture an automobile, and he had helped to train skilled apprentices, among whom was Mr. F. W. Hodges. During Alexander Wilson's time the works were mostly known as 'Wilson's', but as they grew they took the generic name of 'The Vauxhall', which is still much the same today when Vauxhall has a payroll of nearly 36,000. Financial reorganisation in 1897 led to an official title change, to the Vauxhall Iron

Works Company Limited. This reorganisation also brought to the forefront the Alex Wilson & Co. apprentice F. W. Hodges, who put into practice what pioneers like Gardner and others had talked about—the building of a Vauxhall Iron Works automobile.

In this he was aided by a man who, because of his position might have been thought to be unlikely to support such advanced ideas—Mr. J. H. Chambers, the Official Receiver appointed in 1896 to help reorganise the concern financially.

It is common knowledge the world over that before building the first Royce car in 1902, Henry Royce privately purchased a Decauville and drove it around Manchester and his home at Knutsford to gather engineering experience. However, it is not so well known that F. W. Hodges did exactly the same at The Vauxhall. Recalls Darbyshire: 'A car was obtained and thoroughly examined and studied, with the idea of eventually producing an independent and improved design. The model examined had its engine at the rear, tube ignition and a belt drive. How far that sample was responsible for the first car built at the Vauxhall works will probably never be known, but it certainly bore no relation to the original Vauxhall put on the market.' The car probed by Hodges may have been a Benz.

Royce's first experimental car, registration mark M 612, was given its first engine-bench testing on 16th September, 1903. So far as can be determined, it was preceded by some months by the Vauxhall engine.

In *Autocar*'s special supplement 'The Vauxhall Story', published in May, 1969, it was stated that 'Alexander Wilson, founder of the Vauxhall Iron Works, designed that first 1903 car as a tiller-steering two-seater with a single-cylinder 5 h.p. engine and, of the 43 built, only one is known to have survived. It is in London's Science Museum. . . .' We know now that by fortunate chance two of these cars exist: further, Alexander Wilson had left Vauxhall a full seven years before his former

B

apprentice Hodges was experimenting with various engines designed for stationary work and possible use in a car.

One such power unit was a small single-cylinder engine with two opposed pistons. Hodges tried this out in his own river launch *Jabberwock*, and it gave sufficiently good results for him to get the firm's backing for a prototype car engine. Next came a complete car which (according to Darbyshire research) was very much on the lines of subsequent models, but was never developed beyond a few test runs. About this time a five-cylinder radial engine was built and run experimentally, although cooling and lubricating problems defeated it.

'Back to the drawing board' . . . and to the more conventional single-cylinder unit which accounts (and production engineers, too, had they existed at this era) would say was a far better economic proposition. A pioneer craftsman Mr. Harry Pratt, who bored that single cylinder for that first Vauxhall, retired in 1946, after 50 years' service and died in 1964, aged 93.

By the summer of 1903 the little car was running around Lambeth, and *The Autocar* of that October announced: 'The car is steered by a comfortably placed tiller actuated by the left hand. The aim of the designer had been to produce a light car, propelled by mechanism of the simplest character controlled in the simplest manner. . . . We think we may congratulate the makers of the Vauxhall light car upon having designed and turned out a neat, efficient and cheap vehicle which should find many friends.' Its cost was £150.

This report is a reminder that whereas the first Karl Benz car was a Benz, the first Daimler a Daimler, the first Royce a Royce, and so on, the first Rover was not a Lewis, nor the first Vauxhall a Wilson, a Hodges nor a Chambers.

Vauxhall's specification was as follows: 'Its one cylinder of 4-in. bore and $4\frac{3}{4}$-in. stroke is horizontal. It has a governor on the exhaust valve, operated by the foot, and a throttle control on the tiller column. Its two forward speeds are operated by a device on this steering column. No reverse gear was fitted because the car was intended to weigh less than 5 cwt (560 lb), and the law did not require reverse gear to be fitted to cars under that weight. In point of fact this first Vauxhall car exceeded the limit by nearly 50 lb. Suspension is by vertical coil springs, one at each corner of the body. Leaf-springing had been in use for horse-carriages for many years, but coil-springs were probably adopted to save space and weight.'

While the very first Vauxhall was undoubtedly a light car (a category then as different from the rich man's heavy sedanca as a Lambretta now is from a Lamborghini), wealthy patrons of the Vauxhall Iron Works tried to interest Hodges and Chambers in town-carriage styles. In particular, the Earl of Ranfurly proposed a type of hansom-cab body on the 5 hp chassis, the controls being led to a driver's seat high up at the rear. At least one of these was built. As a further way to have the chauffeur and passengers separated (as was invariably the case with horse-drawn carriages), coachbuilders experimented with a town car in which the passengers were housed in a hansom-cab-like structure at the rear, the driver sitting out over the engine-housing, completely unprotected from the elements. One version of this, with the registration mark LC 3363, had solid rear tyres, pneumatics at the front. On the Continent Mercedes had set the pace with the now-orthodox automobile design, as distinct from the Benz dog-cart or motorised horse-carriage, and by 1905 coachbuilders stopped experimenting with eccentric fashions on Vauxhall chassis.

Immediate success came to the first generation of Vauxhalls. The Luton Company still has the original certificate awarded in 1903 by the Wolverhampton & District Automobile Club, stating that: 'Mr. A. G. Price successfully drove a 5 hp Vauxhall car No. 4 weighing 701 lb with two passengers weighing 330 lb up the above (Hermitage Hill, Wolverhampton) in 5 min. 46 sec. on Saturday 24th October, 1903.' A few months later a letter appeared in *The Autocar* from a satisfied customer, Dr. F. C. H. Home, of Egham Hill. 'The wear and tear driving at 15 mph is, in my opinion, almost of negligible quantity', he wrote in May, 1904. 'The average cost of running [daily] has worked out one-third that of the upkeep of my horse . . . I have never at present experienced a moment's worry on the road. . . . The whole of the working parts are attended to by me personally, who am not and never was in any sense a mechanic. . . . An inexpensive, reliable and comfortable means of locomotion, say I.'

Although the first model introduced was primarily a runabout the next model, finalised in February, 1904, was increased in weight by 112 lb, and reverse gear incorporated now as a legal requirement. There were two forward speeds, artillery wheels (spoked) were used in place of the original 1902–3 wire wheels; and the tiller was replaced by the now-conventional steering-wheel in a further model introduced in September, 1904.

Before the tiller was abandoned for the production cars, however, Percy Kidner (Managing Director) aided by F. W. Hodges, entered the 6 hp model in the Glasgow-to-London Run, and the 600-mile Light Car Trials. This helped to prove the superiority of what, more than 60 years later, *Motor* was to describe in its November, 1968, 'Vauxhall Owners' Supplement' as 'a line of crude single-cylinder tiller-steered contraptions'.

With P. C. Kidner in charge, the 6 hp Vauxhall did well in the Glasgow–London Run, being the smallest car entered, and during the entire Trial it lost only seven marks out of 1,000. Those seven marks were lost at the rate of a mark a minute for diagnosing a suspected electric fault and changing a plug. At Woodcock Hill, Barnet, there was a severe test, based on formula including laden and unladen weight, length of the hill, speed and other factors. The Vauxhall crested the hill non-stop in 1 min. 29 sec., at an average speed of 2 mph. Others cars were forced to a halt, but the little 6 hp car was inside the specified limit, and no marks were lost. *The Autocar* gave it special mention for overall performance in the Trial, which incidentally was accomplished at a fuel consumption of 38·25 mpg. One wonders how many present-day trials drivers would like to handle such a mini-power tiller-steered vehicle from Scotland to London. For two days the car did well in the 600-mile Light Car Trials, especially on hills, but on the third day a connecting-rod broke.

F. W. Hodges may have felt the 6 hp model was under-powered, and that anyway Vauxhall Iron Works could do better financially from a vehicle larger than a runabout. He was now designer-director, and while Percy Kidner was chasing back from Scotland, Hodges was testing a prototype of his new 12/14 hp model, to be marketed in November, 1904.

This larger car had three cylinders, water-cooled and sep-arately jacketed, three forward speeds and, of course, reverse, as well as wheel steering. The price-tag was £375, including side and rear paraffin lamps, tyres, pump and repair outfit— all these being extras on many other car-manufacturers' lists.

In their first full year of car production Vauxhall Iron Works built and sold approximately 40 cars. During 1904 they sold 76. Larger premises were needed than the untidy-looking factory at Vauxhall Walk. Wilson built his marine engines on a quarter-acre site, and the first cars were assembled by some 200 men, in a one-acre factory. In those days many local authorities were offering inducements to industry to move. A three-acre site was available at Luton, which had a unique advantage. The local straw-hat industry employed mostly female labour, so there was a surplus of male labour in the town. Luton had just completed its own new municipal electricity supply station. Land was cheap. Rates were low.

The move to Luton was settled some time in 1904, and the move made in 1905. Luton is still regarded as the spiritual head of Vauxhall, although, of course, since the start of the first major post-war expansion in 1949 Vauxhall has spent more than £156 million on enlarging its production capacity of Luton and other centres such as Dunstable, Ellesmere Port, Bedford, and the 700-acre proving ground at Millbrook. In fact Luton's home factory produces nearly all of the models in the range of Vauxhall passenger cars, and Vauxhall/Bedford products are assembled in 18 plants around the world from crated (CKD—'completely knocked down') shipments sent from Britain.

Today as part of the world-wide General Motors organisation, Vauxhall have assembly plants as remote from Luton as South Africa, Australia and New Zealand. However, it is nothing new to Vauxhall to be a success in the export business. One of the 1904 models costing 130 guineas was sold to a pioneer automobilist in Wellington, and this car put up remarkable results in a New Zealand hill-climb in 1908.

2

Luton, Then

Nowadays, when Luton's great press-shops can turn out 16 million pressings in a single month, and Vauxhall as a whole can produce over 700 passenger cars in a single day, it is almost a comic contrast to reflect that throughout the entire year of 1905 they built only 20 cars.

This was worse than a third the 1904 production, and was due to three factors. First, there was the flirtation with eccentric ideas which soon had to be dropped, such as the tourer (one bearing the registration mark BW 289 is a good example) with hood and vertical windscreen—ideas all a little before their time, unpopular, and so were abandoned. Second, there was F. W. Hodges' preoccupation with a new light car to follow his 12/14 model. This was not, as might be expected, a variant on the original 5 and 6 hp models, but a 7/9 hp car with a three-cylinder engine (3-in. bore, $3\frac{3}{4}$-in. stroke) which was in some ways a scaled-down version of the 12/14. The price was around £250, cheaper than the £375 12/14, but still much more expensive than the first Vauxhalls; additionally, there was a tendency to over-body the 7/9 in an attempt to give greater comfort and an appearance of more luxury in a light-car format. By November, 1905, a full-scale 9 hp car was introduced, providing the greater power necessary when tall windscreens were to be forced along the highway. The windscreen was described by one motorist of the period as: 'An abomination always most dangerous when most required', and this may well have been true until the advent of safety glass.

The main reason for the 1905 drop in production was the

move from Vauxhall Walk to Luton. A site of some three acres was purchased—'we were in a factory situated in the middle of fields', records a Vauxhall worker of that day. 'The only other building in sight was a farmhouse'—but, of course, there was delay while plant was moved out from London, buildings and houses were put up. The commentator was not quite correct in saying that the only other building in sight was a farmhouse, for on the other side was the factory of the West Hydraulic Engineering Company which had indirectly been responsible for the move to Luton. For a time it was felt advisable to keep for the move to Luton. For a time it was felt advisable to keep the executive headquarters of Vauxhall in London, but during 1906 the Vauxhall Iron Works amalgamated with their hydraulic neighbours (although not with the farmer, whom they subsequently bought out), and the new firm became known as Vauxhall and West Hydraulic Engineering Company Ltd.

The next big step was the formation of Vauxhall Motors Limited in 1907 to handle the car-making side of the business. Marine engineering continued for some time afterwards, and this arrangement survived in fact until 1914, when the First World War broke out and work was concentrated in military motor vehicles at the growing factory in the Bedfordshire countryside.

However, there are faint historic signs remaining of the 'Hydraulic' days, and still some property built in that era. While researching for this book I was told by a Vauxhall executive: 'If you look carefully enough around this 318-acre site or behind the £1·5 million computer centre you might perhaps come across a little shed where chaps in shirt-sleeves are turning out water pumps, and the whole darned business has grown so vast nobody knows they're still there!' (A harmless joke, in fact, for the 'human relations' side of a huge industrial organisation like Vauxhall Motors doesn't let any facet of the 36,000 or so people at their three main plants escape attention. Nor do the unions.)

Above. Vauxhall pleasure gardens, Lambeth, which were closed in 1859, two years after the founding, nearby, of Vauxhall Ironworks Ltd.

Below. Prospect of Detroit in the 1820's, today the world's greatest motor city. Vessel in foreground is the steam-powered *Walk-in-the-Water*.

Above. First petrol (gasoline) engine made at the Vauxhall Iron Works at the end of the 1890's was installed in Mr. F. W. Hodge's launch *Jabberwock*. It was a single-cylinder engine with two opposed pistons, and formed the basis for the first car engine of 1901/2.

Below. Photo from Vauxhall archives, showing a range of early cars up to 1907. The car on extreme right is in fact the 1903 model.

Above. Motor hansom-cab produced by Vauxhall in 1905 to a design suggested by the Earl of Ranfurley, the chauffeur having steering-wheel and controls at the rear.

Below. Frenzied scene at Brooklands, 1913, when A. J. Hancock captured eleven world's records.

Above. Boyd Edkins at the wheel of his 16/20 hp Vauxhall on which he broke the Melbourne–Sydney record at an average speed of 34 mph for 570 miles, in 1916.
Below. Accompanied by Spahis, General Allenby makes a triumphant entry into Jerusalem in his 25 hp staff car. T. E. Lawrence mentions a green Vauxhall in *The Seven Pillars of Wisdom*.

Production continued at the Luton works despite problems of shifting everything out from London, and by the 1905 Motor Show there were three models on view—the 9 hp and 12/14 three-cylinder cars, and the four-cylinder 18 hp model. It was in this year, too, we have the first record of Mr. A. J. Hancock as a racing driver. In the Isle of Man T.T. he drove a 12/14, but had the bad luck to break a rear wheel while cornering, fortunately with only minor injury to himself. Hancock went on to gain many international records for Vauxhall, helping to introduce the Prince Henry model, and being the first to cover a flying half-mile at 100·08 mph in a 20 hp Vauxhall. Hancock and Percy Kidner piloted Vauxhalls in an astounding record of successes in these early years, and helped to put the name in the category, later to be followed by Sunbeam, Bentley and other marques 'wearing the green'.

What was life really like for the men who built the first Vauxhalls? Today's union members and Vauxhall motorists must be amazed at the contrasts over 60 years.

Among the few able to give an accurate picture was Mr. E. W. Hancock, O.B.E., M.I.Mech.E., F.R.S.A., who worked at Luton in 1911, was Works Manager of Daimler, and eventually became a Rootes Group director and one of the great leaders of the British motor industry. He started as an apprentice with the 'Vauxhall and West Hydraulic'. This part of his life story was told in 'A Lifetime in Automobile Production' in *Automobile Engineer*, from which the relative quotations are extracted.

'We apprentices walked to the factory, started work at 6 am and finished at 5 pm,' he said. 'On top of this we had three evenings per week at what we called "night school". Individual initiative was essential for survival. . . . My first introduction to production was in the tool stores, where very early in life I learnt many things: I soon discovered that while a request for a left-handed spanner was a leg-pull, if I was asked for a pair of footprints I was expected literally to jump to it and produce the real tool.

'In those days machines were virtually used as roughing-out tools for removing the main weight of surplus material from very rough castings or solid forgings. The finished tools were those manipulated by hand: after the hacksaw and hammer and chisel had been used, the final operations were done with the file and scraper. So far as the skilled workers were concerned, the marker-off was the key man, since the success of the job depended primarily on his interpretation of the drawing, and one of the heights of an apprentice's ambition then was to go on the marking-off table. . . .'

Precisely how were these early Vauxhall cars made? Starting at the marking-off table (says Mr. Hancock) each part was individually marked off, and scribed lines and centre-punch dots were the guide to the machinist. First, the castings and forgings were 'favoured' by the marker-off, to determine the best average of the casting or forging; in fact it frequently was only the skill of the marker-off that saved scrapping a valuable part. If there were more than one of an individual part to be marked off, an accurate template, usually of sheet steel, was made. These templates were treasured possessions of the marker-off, and were locked up or even hidden for safety.

The machinist would set up his casting or forging to the lines or dots, and would always leave a 'witness' of the line or split dot to prove his exact interpretation of the marking-off; and when the fitter took over the machined parts he had to decide his own datum point or line, from which he could work for his assembly.

For example, in lining up crankcase bearings prior to hand-scraping it was necessary to select which bearings he should scrape first to accept the test bar. Of course a five-bearing crankcase presented a much more difficult task for ultimate accuracy than a three-bearing case. Then the actual crankshaft that was to be fitted to the crankcase was offered up; the fitting of one to the other took a long time, and it was quite an event when the shaft was finally married to the case. Then, if the crankshaft could be turned by a lever less than two feet in length, it was too slack for running-in.

In those days the individual fitter was usually held responsible for the complete assembly, so when the engine was eventually finished it was passed to the Test section—first for running-in and a subsequent stripping down, final scraping and adjustment. After this the unit would be installed in a chassis, which was passed to the running shed.

Then a further process of testing took place, mainly to run the chassis on the road so that certain units, according to the whim or the skill of the tester, could then be stripped, adjusted and re-tested.

From the beginning to the end—that is, from the fitter to the final tester—there was a gradual increase in the application of individual skills, readjusting, bedding-in and refining. Each car was individual and different, and none of the mechanical components was interchangeable, so they all had to be fitted very carefully. In those days one could pick out a good car for a special customer; it was necessary to bear in mind that he, or his chauffeur, was a mechanic at heart, if not in fact, and that each car had to satisfy different customers in different ways. Body shapes and sizes were fashioned to suit individual requirements, and the customer, who would visit the works from time to time to inspect the body, would often have alterations carried out.

It was customary for the car chassis to be driven to the coachbuilder for the body virtually to be tailored to it, the frame of the body being individually fitted and assembled on it. When the wooden framework was completed the hand-beaten sheet-metal panels were pinned on (later this operation was one of the major causes of disagreement, on lines of demarcation, in factories other than Vauxhall), and finally the bonnet and wings were made and fitted.

Now the chassis, which had been the pride of the road-tester, was standing covered with wood chippings, pieces of sharp jagged sheet metal and filings, and looking very untidy. Of course, it was waiting for the day when the coachbuilder would complete his task and let the running-shed staff take over once more for the final test. How noisy had become the rear axle and the gearbox, how full of creaks and rattles the body! Once more the process of a new and peculiar skill in road-testing gradually reduced these noises to an acceptable or at least an 'as-good-as-you-can-get-it' standard. Then the great day came, and the car was demonstrated, and handed over to the customer.

In the machine-shop the first move towards mechanical re-petition methods of production, and towards intrinsic accuracy, was the use of jigs and special tools, and new methods of meas-urement. Then the use of limits on accuracy in the machine-shop and the improved accuracy of machine tools gave the fitters a more consistent job to work on.

This change started before 1914, when the marker-off had moved back into the tool-room, to mark off castings and forgings for jigs, tools and gauges: by this time, the advent of planning engineers and the issue of process operation sheets led to the establishment of logical sequences of operations, al-though for some years the operation sheets were used only as a general guide. The fitter, with all his skills, files and scrapers, also moved back into the tool-room. His beautifully made hand-scraped bearings were now used to carry the main spindles of machine tools capable of producing, by the thousand, com-ponents to the same degree of accuracy. Parts were being made interchangeable, and were fitted to each other by measurement, instead of by feel.

'After the war', says Mr. Hancock, 'the manufacturing techniques in respect of the mechanical components moved ahead much faster than those for the production of bodies: in fact, car bodies were still being made in much the same way as before the war. Gradually, however, new ideas were introduced. One body-shop with which I was associated started to make the wooden body-members on jigs, and in batches, jig-drilled one side of the half-joints. Assembly jigs were also used, so that all the wooden frame members could be glued and held together, and the wood-screws driven in by a Yankee brace; this made it possible to assemble the body in a separate shop, to consistent dimensions, for mounting on the chassis elsewhere. I even remember a paper on the fallacy of the use of jigs in body-building being presented to a professional institution!

'But gradually competition on the one hand, and improved vehicle performance on the other, made it necessary to give more attention to the body, which therefore came to be considered as part of the complete structure, and not just an afterthought. . . . There was great excitement when the first all-steel body made its appearance, and I remember a car of this type being rolled over down a slope, and then driven away, to demonstrate its safety. . . . It was during the period after the First World War that we produced at Vauxhall Motors the prototype of the Ricardo six-cylinder single-sleeve-valve engine, and the Wilson epicyclic gearbox. . . .'

Without this latter development the birth of the completely automatic transmission would have been delayed, perhaps never conceived. And this important development took place at Luton.

John Alden, C.Eng., F.I.Mech.E., M.S.A.E., has spent most of his working life at Vauxhall, and finally became Director of Engineering in the early 1960s when that other great Vauxhall director and Chief Engineer, Maurice Platt, M.Eng., retired. Platt, who worked with me on *The Motor*, was Chief Engineer at Luton from 1953 to 1963, and succeeded Mr. C. E. King, who was Chief Draughtsman for Vauxhall until his top executive appointment in 1919. All these great engineer-designers, however, bow to 'LHP', L. H. Pomeroy, who joined Luton at the very beginning and was Chief Engineer from 1912 until his retirement in 1919. Father of author Laurence R. Pomeroy, he was the designer of many distinguished Vauxhall models, none more illustrious than the 3-litre Prince Henry which is dealt with in a later chapter, and which surely deserves the title of the first British production sports car.

In the pioneer days of Luton, however, L. H. Pomeroy's first important contribution was the 12/16 four-cylinder car, a very different animal from the Hodges three-cylinder vehicle. It was the first of its type to have a live rear axle (all preceding models were chain-driven), and it really heralded the bigger, more powerful cars that brought sporting success to future Vauxhalls, for example, by 1908 the 20 hp four-cylinder Vauxhall began a long series of successes in a team headed by Percy Kidner. In the RAC and Scottish Trials of that year it became the first car in the world to complete 2,000 miles without involuntary stop.

To the present generation of Vauxhall motorists the Pomeroy designs in general and the 18 hp four-cylinder model in particular are important because it was on this the famous fluted radiator and bonnet (hood) were introduced. Every Vauxhall produced from 1906 to 1959 had this very distinctive bonnet-flute design until at the beginning of the 1960's it became impossible to incorporate the flutes in conjunction with modern styling. Of course, there have been changes through the years. For instance, the original flute was continued through the whole length of the bonnet to the dashboard, and did not taper. A break from the parallel lines came with the original 1910 C-type Vauxhall. By 1913 the 30/98—the most famous Vauxhall of those historic days—had tapered flutes, and so the style continued until 1959.

How did it start? There had always been reticence about it at Luton, and it is common knowledge that at times various Chief Engineers and stylists felt it was a heavy cross to bear! A Luton historian told me: 'The idea of the flutes came to one of our directors in 1906 whilst lying in bed contemplating a shield design carved on his wardrobe. He was so struck by its suitability for the frontal design of a car that he insisted it should be adopted for Vauxhall.'

3

Luton, Now

At the wheel of his Viva, Victor, Ventora, Cresta or Viscount—or even at the wheel of an earlier Velox, G-type, Cadet, 'Silent 80' R-type 20/60 or classic 30/98—any Vauxhall motorist of the generation after the First World War may wonder what the link is between Luton in the Vauxhall and West Hydraulic Engineering days and the multi-million Luton of today.

It is therefore instructive in this Vauxhall story to step in imagination for a moment from the picture so far given of the pioneering days, to the vast complex of Luton, which is the registered office and administration headquarters.

At the other two major manufacturing plants there is also a huge daily production. The Bedford truck plant at Dunstable is capable of building more than 300 goods-vehicle chassis every 24 hours; and at Ellesmere Port, on Merseyside, Vauxhall Motors currently build fourteen of the models in the 20-model Viva range. Ellesmere Port also produces many mechanical units for Luton and Dunstable.

Millions who have never owned a Vauxhall car are still very familiar with the Vauxhall plant, since the main road to Luton Airport winds its way through the heart of the 318-acre complex. However, they do not realise that in the Bedfordshire countryside a few miles from Luton is the research and test-centre at Chaul End. This 58-acre site is still a most important part of the facilities available to the Engineering Department, even though there is now (since 1969) a 700-acre proving site at Millbrook, about 18 miles north of Luton.

Luton has been the home of Vauxhall for well over 60 years,

as we have seen, and in that time the firm and the town have grown up together. Throughout the 24 hours on various shifts there are always around 19,000 men and women in Luton trekking to The Vauxhall, or returning at the end of a stint. They have helped to design, build, test or deliver Victor saloon and estate cars, the Ventora, the Cresta and Viscounts, Viva estates and van models.

This chapter can be read by anyone visiting Luton to see Vauxhall at work, and is a supplement to the well-illustrated booklet which Michael Marr's minions issue to every visitor, VIP or ordinary member of the public. About 20,000 people each year visit Vauxhall at Luton, and they see everything from the great press-shops to the electrostatic paint-spraying plant, the precision machining, assembly lines, and are initiated into some of the secrets of Quality Control audit procedures. What visitors cannot so readily appreciate is the vast investment by Vauxhall in its three major plants. Since 1949 Vauxhall Motors has spent more than £150 million on enlarging and improving production capacity.

One part of the Luton plant not included in the visitor's tour is the Engineering and Styling Centre discussed in detail in a later section of this book. This centre, completed at the end of 1964 at a cost of £2¼ million (about $5 million) divides into sections, dealing with styling and engineering, and when visitors ask their guides why this ultra-modern Detroit-like building is on the Top Secret list it is explained: 'This is because the people working there are busy on vehicles that will be announced four or more years ahead, and we do like to keep to ourselves what our future cars are going to look like!'

The other tangible reason for security is that research, styling and testing are the result of an enormous capital investment. It can cost up to £30,000 to produce one working prototype of an advanced model and for marketing reasons advance designs are kept confidential.

C

Of course, the whole key to Luton is steel. It arrives by road in bales and coils. Supplies of sheet steel and plate alone, in a single month, can total over 12,000 tons, and at Luton automatic guillotines cut up the material into required lengths, ready for the presses.

Production really begins in the press-shop, where the sheet and coil steel is pressed into the various panels that go to make up car bodies. The main shop at Luton is a lofty, noisy, well-lit windowed hall housing about 250 presses, some of them giant machines weighing over 300 tons, towering 30 feet into the cathedral-like roof, and exerting pressures of 1,500 tons. A smaller separate press-shop produces panels for Bedford truck and van bodies, and together these turn out 16 million pressings a month. Ellesmere Port has its own press shop.

Despite the heavy material and the enormous pressures involved, work in the press-shops is not hazardous. The presses stand in rows, each line producing one type of pressing non-stop. Pressed panels are lifted out by what the operatives call 'iron hands', and moved automatically in the correct position to the next press in the line. Other presses, producing smaller components such as hub-caps, are fed with large coils of steel strip which is cut up and the pieces passed from one set of dies to the next, all in the same huge press. Each of the eleven bays in this press-shop has an overhead crane, and the steel-stores area is served by three more.

Below the main floor-level is a system of chutes and conveyors along which travel all the steel off-cuts from the presses above. This scrap is delivered to a huge baling machine and eventually returned to the steel mills to be melted down and re-processed.

Some first time Luton visitors are fascinated by the enormous size and power of the presses which thud through day and night, while others are intrigued by the big presses which are also transfer machines, performing 10 or more operations in automatic sequence. Occasionally a visitor will complain:

'But this is all stuff for *new* cars. I drive a four-year-old estate job, and I've been waiting weeks for a replacement part.'

With around 300,000 vehicles a year coming out of all three plants, it certainly is an additional responsibility to

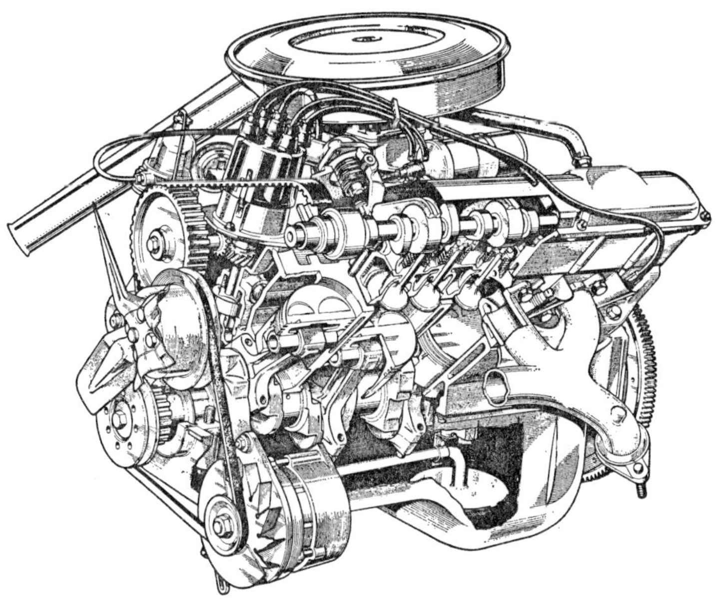

Cutaway drawing of the Victor and Victor 2000 engine, first introduced in 1967 for 1968 models. The virtually indestructible toothed rubber belt which drives the overhead camshaft can be seen at the left. The four-in-line cylinders are inclined at an angle of 45-degrees.

manufacture spares. There is no separate area of the plant for this. As well as producing the pressings needed for normal daily car production (this can total as many as 800,000 a day), the press-shops also turn out an increasing volume of pressings destined to serve as replacement parts for current and non-current models.

From the press-shops the components pass into the body-shop, and to the newcomer this is perhaps the most dramatic aspect of Luton. The 'gate-line' section of the mammoth shop shows embryo cars for the first time (the odd shapes coming from the presses in their raw state are almost impossible to determine), and it is a continuous fireworks display when major sub-assemblies are clamped together and welded to form the rigid body shell.

A car body is really made up of six units—the floor, two sides, front-end, rear-end, and the roof. Despite all the expertise of the stylists, the result is still essentially a sheet-steel box, albeit streamlined and styled so that the lines flow. These six major sections are themselves made up from a number of smaller pressings, and these reach the main body-building conveyor as sub-assemblies from the subsidiary feed conveyors. Unusually-shaped trucks, moving along a floor conveyor, carry the body floor assembly; pairs of heavy frames holding the sides, front and rear sections, mate up with the trucks so that all the units are clamped securely together before the start of welding. The roof is the last of these major sections to go on. Welding alone will not necessarily produce a water-tight body, so each single joint is sealed with a hard-setting compound capable of withstanding considerable temperature variations. There is a rigorous watertight test much later in the production sequence.

Seam-welding and spot-welding are the two main forms of weld used in building up Vauxhall body shells, and one single body shell contains up to 5,200 individual spot-welds, and as many as 300 inches of 'live' welding by CO_2 and oxy-acetylene. Some of the huge multi-spot welding machines in this Luton shop, three times the height of a man, make a large number of simultaneous spot-welds in a few seconds.

It is a magnificent panorama, since as many as 400 body shells pass through this shop at one time on conveyors with a total length of about three miles.

When the shells have collected their doors, bonnet panels and boot lids, they are prepared for the paint-shop next door,

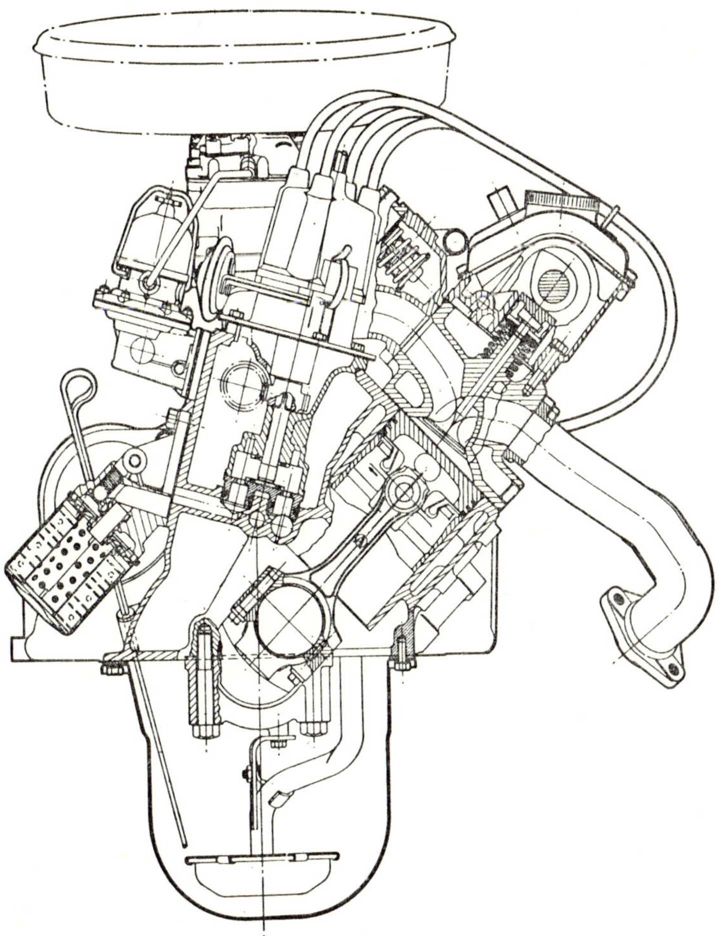

Mid-cross-section of the Victor and Victor 2000-series engine. There are two versions, 1,599 c.c. (97·5 cu.in) and 1,975 c.c. (120·5 cu.in). The hemispherical combustion chambers are fully machined. The overhead camshaft acts directly on the valves through inverted bucket-type tappets.

panel surfaces being inspected and blemishes in the sheet metal removed with portable sanding machines. This is all part of the hand craftsmanship which goes into making a motor-car even in the largest and most-automated plant. In the same way there is more to painting car bodies than just spraying them with a coat of shining bright paint. At this stage in the Luton production line, 'painting' means protection of the sheet metal, inside and out, underneath as well as on top. More than seven gallons of protective paints and finishes are applied to a single Vauxhall body, with some of the models, and the Luton paint shop alone uses over 4,000 gallons of paints and finishes every 24 hours.

Every side of the motor industry in Britain, Continental Europe and the United States has suffered from industrial disputes, many of which have dominated television bulletins and documentaries, and made Press headlines. Naturally the two greatest groups in the world, headed by General Motors, of which Vauxhall has been a part since 1925, bore the brunt of these problems, and so past headlines such as 'Vauxhall Violence' (1966), 'Vauxhalls Crack Down' (1967), 'Car Plant to Shut' (1968) and 'Viva Production Lines Halt as Talks Break Down' (1969) are remembered by millions of the general public, since they can identify the human problems with an individual make of car. The same is not true for the steel suppliers of the great component manufacturers, including Girling, Lucas and Armstrong. As many people visiting Luton and the other Vauxhall production centres have their own views about labour relations, and may well have been involved in strikes themselves, there is a natural and possibly not unhealthy interest in the production lines at Luton in general and in the vast paint-shop in particular, for industrial trouble here during 1966 started heartbreaks in a works which had always had the best labour relations in the trouble-torn motor industry. There were problems in the paint-shop all throughout 1966, and it cannot be denied that many

Luton visitors are curious to know not only how Vauxhalls are painted but what it was in this shop which triggered off the troubles.

On a factual basis, no hint can be gleaned as to why there should at that time have been poor labour relations in the shop. No matter whether a Luton visitor subscribes to the 'Make-the-workers-work' philosophy or regards all industrial bosses as 'Lick-spittle running dogs of the neo-Fascist Society' (typical phrases overheard as frequently at Luton as in Coventry, Dagenham, Dearborn or Detroit during the heat of a strike), no obvious reason for distress comes from a visit to the mammoth Luton paint-shop. The old-time problems of spraying being dirty work do not apply in any sense of an industrial dispute.

Later we will look closer at Vauxhall's fine human-relations schemes, but facts become distorted or forgotten, and the truth becomes buried. The industrial dispute is today as much a built-in aspect of the car industry as is a Churchill tool or a 1,500-ton steel press. As strikes, disputes and delays affect car deliveries and overall costs, the customer visiting Luton—or any other major car factory—is very concerned to know what goes wrong, even though he may be reluctant to ask the questions aloud. A true picture was given by a national Press commentator in October, 1966: 'The angry mob scenes round Vauxhall Motors works at Luton were as stupid as they were depressing. Banging the sides of trucks, shouting mindless anti-American slogans and unhitching trailers is no way to get a point over. . . .'

As already mentioned in the Acknowledgement section of this book, the comments and opinions here expressed are mine, and do not necessarily in any way express the Company viewpoint.

A London *Daily Mail* leader explained that these troubles came on top of the four-day week brought in as the result of government financial squeeze, and that the dispute was: 'blown up into a rampage against American management'.

'One paint shop official' (said the leader-writer) 'claims that Vauxhall makes £900 a year profit per man employed. This is being compared unfavourably with £600 a year for Ford and £300 a year for a British motor group. What is unfavourable about that? It shows that Vauxhall is efficiently managed. It helps to explain why when thousands of workers are being sacked in other parts of the industry, Vauxhall has promised no redundancies . . . . There are also complaints about the £7½ million of last year's profit that went back as dividends to the General Motors parent in the US. But General Motors is also investing more that £50 million in Vauxhall's expansion plans over the next five years. That is what the profit is being used for. . . .'

Well, all troubles are overcome in time, and Vauxhall was recipient of the Queen's Award to Industry for the first time in 1965-6 (a recognition bestowed on only 115 of the 1,000 British companies considered), and in February, 1967, the Company was granted the Royal Warrant as motor-vehicle manufacturers to the Queen. This is all a tribute to the skill and craftsmanship of Vauxhall's workers: and the generally good industrial pattern enabled the chairman David Hegland to announce that of the new cars sold in Britain in July, 1969, one in every six was a Vauxhall. This is the highest proportion ever recorded, and is surely the factual answer to exaggerated stories of strikes and threatened lock-outs.

The real behind-the-scenes story of the paint-shop is technically more interesting because much of the paint used is acrylic, and it is applied in a line-production method known as the 'sand-and-bake' technique. *Autocar*'s Edward Eves went to Luton in 1963, not long after the Fisher Body Corporation (GM) started work on acrylics, which were first used in Britain by Rolls-Royce. However, the reflow process was introduced by Vauxhall, and was entirely new to Britain. Mr. Eves disclosed that the line-production method was: '. . . discovered at the Atlanta, Georgia, plant of General Motors when a batch of bodies was contaminated with grit particles. To save stripping, the bodies were oil-sanded and put back through the drying ovens at a higher temperature than normal, in order to melt the finish and make it flow into the minute scratches produced by rubbing-down. To the surprise of one and all, the finish achieved was much better than before. This set off a line of research into baking temperatures which ended up with the process which Vauxhall and other GM plants now favour.'

This 'lucky discovery' culminates at Luton in a long series of paint-shop processes, the first of which is a seven-part rust-proofing, followed by almost complete immersion of the body shell in a 5,000-gallon tank of primer. Next come two full coats of acrylic primer surfacer, including a very high-pressure application to the entire underbody, the wheel-arches and the insides of the body-sills. This primer is then baked in huge high-temperature ovens. All the while the shells are moved on metal-link conveyors, gliding along in much the same way as a car passes through a garage machine-wash.

After the first baking the entire underbody and wings receive a thick coating of tough bituminous compound which serves the dual purpose of protecting the sheet metal and reducing road noise in finished cars. Finally, each shell receives four full coats of the finish colour, in high-lustre acrylic paint. Electrostatic spraying was introduced in the Vauxhall paint shops. With this process a potential is applied to the metal shell, and this charge 'draws' the paint rather like a magnet attracting metal. There is plenty of scope for craftsmanship in the shop, for the final coats are applied by manual spray guns which help to cover areas that may have been lightly sprayed by the automatic equipment. They say there are 20 miles of pipes at Luton through which pass the paints, primers, sealers and other materials.

Although they are still only painted body shells, the panels now begin to resemble complete cars. The next stage is the trim-shop, a series of long avenues lit by rows of brilliant strip-lamps like an array on a motorway underpass tunnel. Each body shell makes a 4,000-foot journey by conveyor belt through the trim-shop, where they collect the scores of components ('furnishings' is the trade term) that turn them into car bodies. The conveyor carries 250 shells at one time, taking them through a large number of 'stations' where the various items are fitted, including carpets, seats, door-handles, window glass, chrome trim mouldings, electric wiring, steering-wheels, facia panels and a host of other items. Many 'furnishings' fed to this main trim conveyor are made up on the spot, in subsidiary brilliantly lit areas ranged along the huge trim-shop— including seats, door-trim panels, instrument clusters and so on.

Midway through this long furnishing process, when all the glass is in place in the shell, comes a water tunnel. As each body passes through, it is drenched from every angle by water jets. In fact the water contains a flourescent dye, and an ultra-violet lamp is used to detect any drop of water finding its way into the body shell. There is no particular Luton uniform, and men work in dungarees, overalls or in shirt-sleeves as they wish and according to the weather; however, all along this trim conveyor (as in other production areas) the white-coated inspectors of the Quality Control department are stationed. Vauxhall have spent £300,000 building a new Quality Control centre, which few casual Luton visitors see as there just is not enough time on the stock factory day visit. But it is not an idle publicity line to say that the centre is the 'nerve-centre of all the Company's efforts to maintain the highest standards in car and commercial-vehicle production'.

The 1,100 staff of the whole 'R. and QC' network range from the Quality Control and Reliability Manager down to the many inspectors in all the factory manufacturing areas, and the same is true at Dunstable and Ellesmere Port.

This division is responsible for the accuracy of all tools,

jigs, fixtures and equipment used to produce car and truck components. Their work starts with the arrival of the first component for assembly. Samples, whether from outside sources or from within the plant, have to conform to specification, which includes metallurgical and chemical acceptance, covering the range from paint to plastics, from felt to forgings, from carpet to castings. Nowhere in the Vauxhall factories do you see manufacturing jobs being done without the white-coated inspectors in attendance; no production materials enter, the plants, and no new vehicle leaves, without Quality Control approval.

Vehicles are regularly selected and subjected to a series of checks by a team known as 'auditors', working for the Reliability department. Their job is to sheck such details as weld faults. This part of the Reliability Audit takes place in Q-Block.

Some research is done in the Chaul End laboratory, where they have X-ray equipment, and other scientific aids using radio-isotopes and optics. One of the most complex tasks in measuring relates to the control of tooth-forms on all types of gear wheels. Precision equipment, for example, measures the helical angles of gears to very fine tolerances. Chemical and metallurgical tests are made on materials entering Luton, and the Quality Control 'audit' even involves checking the tightness of every nut and bolt in a car.

In one area of the Quality Control zone in Luton's V-Block one may find a white-coated inspector cheerfully hacking at a sample body shell with hammer and chisel. While this may at first seem unscientific, the fact is that random shells are taken from the body shop to test the strength of the many welds. In the hands of a man who knows what he is looking for, hammer and chisel are the best tools.

Back in the main production area, the units (finished bodies, now) are lowered from the end of the trim conveyor to the final assembly conveyor which runs along the floor below this area; but before they finally leave the trim shop they collect some minor mechanical units such as shock-absorbers.

So far we have been considering the manufacture of the body, but just as impressive is a large building nearby where the mechanical units are produced. 'Units' in this sense means power-units, gearboxes and transmission systems. Some major units for Luton-built cars—gearboxes, for instance—are manufactured at Ellesmere Port and delivered by road to Luton. Many others, including the advanced overhead-cam engines for Victor models, are produced in this huge Luton machine shop.

The Victor's engine is assembled on a 430-foot-long line having 86 adjustable pedestals, while at the other side of the assembly area is the 'hot test' section, where 28 motoring units are used to run each engine under its own power for 15 minutes while timing and carburation adjustments are made. At the outset, however, castings, stampings and forgings arrive in rough form from outside suppliers, and scores of costly, high-precision machine tools are used at Luton to machine, cut and finish these components. Many of the machine tools have built-in automatic control devices to ensure consistent accuracy and high quality. In recent times an even more sophisticated manufacturing complex has been established at Ellesmere Port, making possible new techniques in engine building, body-building and final assembly.

Major engine components are produced on transfer machines that automatically move a component from one machining station to the next, and some of these transfer machines carry out a hundred operations or more on scores of components *simultaneously*. The Victor overhead-cam block line, for example, consists of 19 in-line transfer machines performing multiple operations in 123 different working stations. All the machines are linked by automatic storage conveyors and loaders which hold some 750 cylinder blocks, and the total number of blocks in the line when it is full is about 1,050. This area of the Luton works is ultra-modern in appearance, presenting a vista of light-grey control desks resembling the launching control of a space satellite. This is duplicated at Ellesmere Port.

Equally impressive are the batteries of gear-cutting machines working to very close tolerances, while in the same building are some of the heat-treatment furnaces in which steel components are hardened, tempered and generally treated to ensure long life, reduced wear and maximum reliability. The whole area is a mass of contrasts, for on the one hand there are the assembly lines with the automated machinery for the Victor engines, somewhat similar lines for the 3·3-litre Cresta/Viscount engines; and on the other hand one comes suddenly on laboratory-type checking desks, where skilled men grade and carefully check each piston, following its tin-plating on an automatic machine, before insertion into the engine blocks.

Of the average of 20,000 visitors to Luton each year, many come more than once. Really this is advisable for the Vauxhall owner who wants to keep in close touch with the centre of it all, for there are constant changes being made to cope with scientific, engineering and styling improvements, to speed production, and to make life easier for operatives. The latest assembly lines at Luton have been installed for production of the 1,600 cc and 2,000 cc overhead cam engines for Victor models. The 1,600 unit is also available as an option on Vivas (built at Ellesmere Port, currently), while the twin-carburetter 2,000 unit powers the Viva GT and the VX 4/90.

Even in the last two sentences several different 'options' have been mentioned; throughout Vauxhall as a whole there is a vast range of engine, transmission, styling, colour and furnishing options, and we are now reaching the stage of production where the finalising of the options becomes very complex.

First, the car body has to meet its mechanical units, and this meeting takes place at one end of the 1,000-foot-long final assembly conveyor on the ground floor of Luton's main car-production building. Engines, gearboxes and axles are delivered by conveyor from the machining areas, while the bodies descend from the trim-shop on the floor above to meet the 'mechanicals'. In a way, this body-drop station is the point at which the jigsaw first looks complete, although the cars need a great deal more work on them before they are finally passed out.

In the body-drop stations shells are lowered on mounting brackets on long shafts, synchronising with the mechanical units supported on a long platform about chest-height from the ground. To the newcomer, a fascinating aspect of this assembly business is the way the correct body shells and mechanicals reach the right place at the right time. Customers' orders, giving details of model, colour and other options, are translated into code-numbers which are then fed by teleprinters to 22 control centres in the main production areas. Thus each area knows the number and sequence of units to be delivered to the final lines.

All the main feeder conveyors, delivering bodies, wheels and tyres, engines, gearboxes and other mechanicals, are synchronised, their speed being set to suit the daily output figure needed. Along this final assembly line there are 61 assembly stations, and numerous Quality Control points as well.

Watch, for a moment, the body-drop from the floor above. The trimmed body meets its front and rear axles, engine, gearbox and wheels in a pre-assembled mechanical unit. Finally the car is driven off the end of the line—under its own power— to undergo a long series of checks and inspections before it leaves the building. Free-running rollers in the floor enable cars to be 'driven' in all gears while inspectors check the functioning of all the mechanicals. At the same time they test lights, flashing indicators, horn and other electricals, and controls.

Every single car goes through the roller test, and the QC men can call for an additional road test or Audit check.

Just as many a visitor to Vauxhall will want to ask some

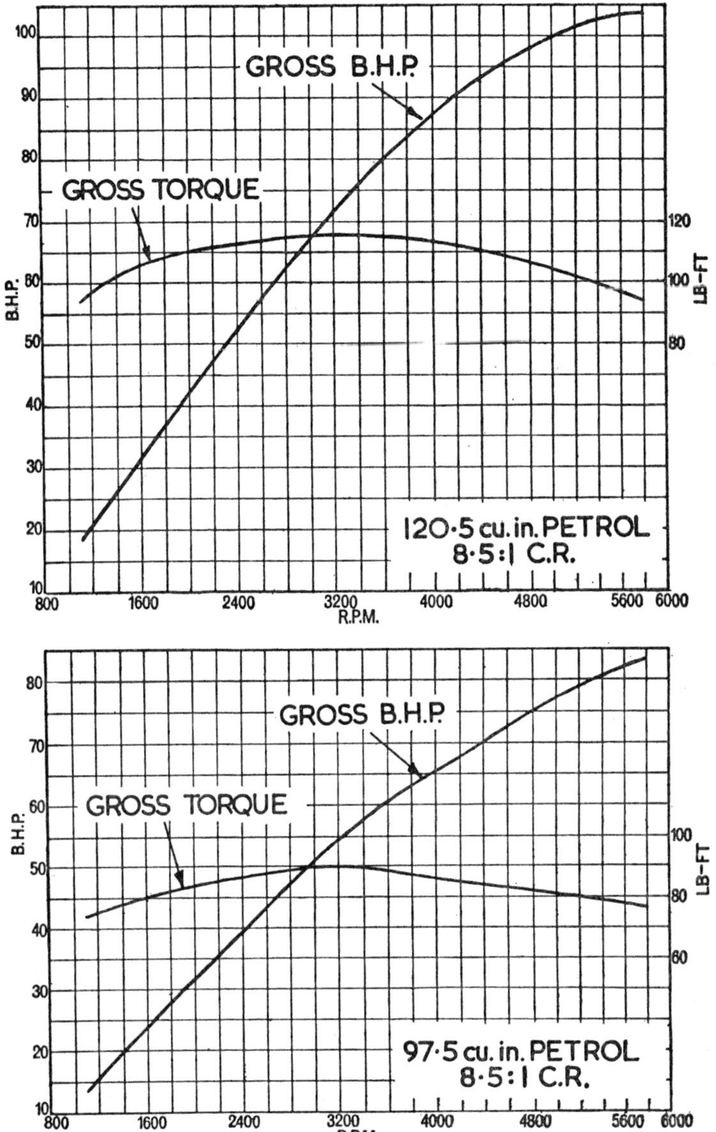

Power curves of the 120·5 and 97·5 cu.in versions of the engine introduced for the Victor series in 1968.

probing questions about industrial relations, so there is always a Vauxhall motorist complaining that he is still awaiting delivery of a spare part, or some lack of communication with his dealer regarding servicing. To see what happens in Parts and Accessories, and in Service, visitors are taken from the main Luton centre to Toddington, which is some four miles away, at Dunstable. Every industry comparable in size and complexity with Vauxhall inevitably finds a small proportion of users with justifiable complaints, and naturally these are more vocal than the satisfied customers.

The astounding position has to be faced frankly that Toddington's Parts and Accessories department sells goods worth over £25,000,000 every year. The man who waits impatiently for a spare fender bracket, or perhaps a wiring harness or a suspension component, can hardly visualise this enormous scope. Every day some 250 tons of parts and accessories are moved out of the huge modern warehouse, and of this daily total about 40 per cent go for export. Stocks of more than 64,000 separate part-numbered items are kept: in all, the warehouse holds about 20 million separate pieces, from nuts and bolts to complete body shells. Shifting such an immense daily quota was a problem not easy to solve but it has been done with an electronic Robotug system which invariably fascinates newcomers to Toddington. They are perplexed at the way the twelve automatically controlled miniature 'electric-train' Robotugs towing long trailers weave their way to any one of fourteen stations in the warehouse. A bright warning-light flashes as the tugs travel safely along invisible tracks between benches of girls wrapping kits of brake-linings, trim accessories and all the rest. Each of the 14 stations in the circuit can handle up to four trains at once, but as the tugs travel only at ground level, there has to be an even more startling facility for dealing with heavy units such as engines and gearboxes needing to be stacked high.

Three aisles of King-Triax automatic storage equipment are

in the new warehouse for holding engines and gearboxes. A single aisle for engines is 30 bays long, with storage on five levels, with capacity for 300 engines. The two gearbox aisles are 18 bays long on eight levels, storing 576 boxes.

It is fascinating watching this robot-like equipment. Retrievers automatically travel between the racks serving both sides of the aisles. Pick-up and discharge stations integrate the whole of this plant (British-built, under an agreement with the Triax Company of USA), and the operatives like the system because of its safety devices. Free-falling protection incorporating slack chain detection is there to arrest the vertical carriage in the event of failure. Vauxhall and Bedford engines are stored on flat plywood pallets over 5 feet long, and there is a King Mytemin hoist over each pick-up and discharge station.

Control of these spare-part retrievers is by plastic punched cards. These are colour-coded for each of the three aisles, and every location has an individual card. While each load is in storage, the relevant paper-work is filed in a transparent pocket on the card serving that particular location. As a load arrives for storage, the operator picks an available opening card for the aisle, puts the paper-work in the pocket, then places the plastic card in the card-reader on the retriever control console. He presses the 'start' button, and the retriever automatically stores the load in the chosen location! To get at a spare, cards are simply taken from the 'loads stored' file, and every load is accessible just by button-pushing. Although the system is entirely automatic from the pressing of the 'start' button, everything can be worked by overriding manual controls.

Computers are used for Vauxhall stock-control and invoicing, and there is a 24-hour phone answering system handling very urgent orders. To minimise delay, Vauxhall have introduced a new Lamson Airtube communications system at Toddington, extended from the original two and a half miles at Dunstable to four and a half miles of strip-steel 4-in. tubing. A hundred transparent carriers are drawn through the tubing at about

D

20 mph (30 feet a second) by 30 hp three-phase motors creating more than two inches of vacuum. Most people seeing this system for the first time imagine it is worked by compressed air; in fact it is powerful vacuum suction.

All this helps to speed deliveries of Vauxhall spares. Perhaps it is only human nature for the man impatiently waiting to get in the post a spare without which his car is immobile to care little about Lamson Airtubes, King Triax storage, or Robotugs. However, only those working in a big export industry realise that in addition to manufacturing and handling the spare part, many irritating twentieth-century frills have to be coped with, such as packing strips, packing notes (domestic), packing and evaluation notes (export), reserve stock requests, receiving and despatch documents, part order corrections and goods-inwards documents, and dealer claims forms.

Dealers, like private owners, need to be kept supplied with information, as well as spare parts, and at Luton there is a Service department which exists primarily to produce and pass on information on after-sales service and maintenance. This information goes to some 1,400 Vauxhall and Bedford dealers in the United Kingdom, and to all GM plants and distributors overseas. Indeed, one of the six major divisions into which this Service department is divided is concerned with the provision of after-sales service in overseas territories, many of them extremely remote. There is the Service Training centre, where dealers' service staffs from all over the world attend training courses; nothing very dramatic to watch, perhaps— just groups of engineers in their trim white uniform jackets watching or working on a Vauxhall unit mounted on a bench. What is of powerful importance, nevertheless, is the fact that to this Luton training centre come annually some 2,000 men from nearly every country in the world, working with a staff of full-time Vauxhall instructors at Luton.

While this main Service Training Centre is at Luton, there

are local training centres at Antrim and Edinburgh. There are also well-appointed service stations which look after Vauxhall's own fleet of cars, vans, trucks and coaches that keep up a shuttle-service between Luton and Ellesmere Port.

From this brief survey of Luton today, we turn back to past Vauxhall glories and international successes, to the immortals like the C-type Prince Henry and the 30/98, to explore Detroit, to the great days of Sir Charles Bartlett, the man who not only brought true motoring craftsmanship to Luton but who left behind him a monument which for so many years kept Vauxhall free from industrial strife. They called it 'MAC' —the Management Advisory Committee, which was set up in 1941 and has been called 'simply an exercise in industrial democracy'. The JNC and other stewards' committees now supervise the MAC.

Human relations may not seem so interesting a subject as motor-cars, but in the present complex world you can't get good cars without good human relations. When you visit Luton or the other plants you begin to learn some of the behind-the-scenes facets—the profit-sharing schemes, medical centres (there are six surgeries at Luton alone), pension and health-insurance schemes, long-service recognition, and apprenticeship, secretarial and management training courses. Because the Vauxhall plants are strongly identified with their places on the map of Britain, Vauxhall employees are encouraged to take part in local affairs and are given paid leave-of-absence for work such as service on borough, urban and rural councils. In a recent year the mayors both of Luton and of Dunstable were Vauxhall employees.

Broadcaster and writer Graham Turner delved into Luton's human relations for his brilliant book *The Car Makers* (Eyre & Spottiswoode) which dealt with statistics and sources of strife in Britain's car industry. He called Vauxhall 'the gold mine on the hill', and commented that the new prosperity resulting from glittering gadgetry had 'injected into Luton a perpetual gold-rush mentality, not so primitive as the Klondyke, but just as acquisitive'. He rightly pointed out that new labour pours in from all over the country, and world. 'Ninety-five per cent of the job-hunters I see are foreigners to Luton,' one foreman told Graham Turner. 'I've got Hungarians, Germans, Swedes, Russians, coloured men—I've even got Wong the Welder.'

Does it all add up to relatively contented men and women building the sort of car that Vauxhall motorists like to drive? Graham Turner had this quote from a shop steward: 'It's a good firm, though God forbid that I should ever say so to their face.'

4

The Sporting Years

In the preceding chapter we momentarily moved on by some 60 years to get an impression of Luton today, as a contrast to the early history of the Iron Works. While the mighty Vauxhall organisation is now world-wide, it must not be overlooked that a generation ago the name of Vauxhall was also illustrious at Brooklands and international Trials.

Vauxhall's sporting years and the development from the early 1900's until 1925 when the Company was acquired by General Motors constitute a saga in themselves, and the development was extremely rapid from 1907 onwards. This was the year when the Luton group found that marine engines and hydraulic machinery were retarding the development of motor-cars, and the decision was made to form Vauxhall Motors Limited to take over all car production, the other work to be continued by the West Hydraulic Engineering concern. Although they remained neighbours for many years, they were now entirely separate entities. This Company change, already mentioned briefly in Chapter 2, was an enormous impetus to Vauxhall, the board now being formed with Leslie Walton and Percy Kidner as joint Managing Directors, and F. W. Hodges as Consulting Engineer. Inspired by Pomeroy, they produced a range of cars of which the first to achieve success was the C-type which continued in production until 1913, and in time to be known as the Prince Henry. It was the first Vauxhall to have en bloc cylinder casting, thermo-siphon cooling and other 'modern' features; the four-speed box was an improvement on that used for the 18 hp car of

1907. Rated horsepower was 20·1 (bore and stroke 90 and 120 mm respectively), the 9 ft. 7 in. wheelbase car was shod with 870 × 100's, and the chassis price was £420. A standard body cost only an extra £45 in those days.

The introduction of this C-type was of outstanding importance to Vauxhall, and historians glean a hint of blunt differences of opinion between Hodges and Pomeroy, whose brainchild the new model was. Pomeroy and Kidner were also more enthusiastic about reliability trials and the commercial value of sporting successes than was Hodges. However, as L. C. Darbyshire recalls, in February 1908 the regulations governing the 2,000-mile RAC Trials were published, and as Hodges was away in Egypt at that time, Pomeroy seized the opportunity to enter a 20 hp for this event. It could be said that this RAC Trial was a spur which aided production of Vauxhall's first successful model. There was opposition to the project from many older members of the firm, and many of the 20 hp car's features were produced under difficult conditions. Pom worked far into the nights completing a 20 hp chassis for the event, and this was complicated by the fact that the RAC rating had not then become standard, and engineers were searching for a formula which all major manufacturers would accept. For a time it seemed it might even be necessary to enter a 12/16 Vauxhall, the 15·9 hp engine of which was 80 × 102 in the standard version, although a few were produced with 85-mm-bore engines rated variously at 17·9 and 18·2 hp.

The 2,000 mile Trial started in London and linked up with the Scottish Reliability Trials in Glasgow. There were some timed hill-climbs in Scotland and the Lake District, and finally a Brooklands speed test of 200 miles. As we have seen in Chapter 2, Percy Kidner drove the 20 hp and completed the whole event with loss of fewer marks than any other car in the Trial, irrespective of class. At the newly opened Brooklands, knowing he had a considerable lead over all cars irrespective of class, Kidner resisted the temptation to risk mechanical failure by a last-minute burst of speed, so the average for the whole distance was 46 mph instead of the 55 mph or thereabouts which could have been obtained. By keeping speed down, however, Kidner chalked up another fine Vauxhall point which impressed the pioneer motoring public, to judge by subsequent correspondence in the technical Press, and this was the low petrol consumption. The 20 hp was fifth in all classes under this heading, averaging 26 mpg as against the top consumption figure of 29·1 mpg obtained with a much smaller 8 hp car.

Anyone who had studied motoring papers of the day and their virulent correspondence columns will know that there was much criticism of the Trial and what it proved. Critics, perhaps silently inspired by rival chief engineers of other companies, complained that Vauxhall's success had been a matter of chance, and this Pomeroy found difficult to deny, since this was the first time his new model had competed. So the only way to thwart criticism was to enter it quickly for other events. This was done, and the car subsequently distinguished itself with a fastest time in the Hertfordshire County AC climb at Aston, at Gaillon in France, and in the Lancashire AC Climb at Rivington Pike. Kidner also won the President's Cup for the best all-round performance at Shelsley Walsh hill-climb that year.

Vauxhall's Aston Clinton success is a reminder of the hill which gave the Aston Martin its name. Lionel Walker Birch Martin was partner with Robert Bamford in an engineering works and they decided jointly to produce a small British sports car. As capital was almost non-existent, they used a sports Singer as a basis for this venture. Dudley Coram in his Motor Racing Publications book *Aston Martin*, pointing out that in 1913 there were no outstanding sports light cars, comments: 'The real sports cars of the day were exemplified by the "Prince Henry" Vauxhall which, though eminently successful was a large expensive vehicle, and it became a matter of extreme interest to Lionel Martin to see if it were possible to step up the performance of the little 10 hp Singer.'

In this Martin and his partner were very successful, and as the Prince Henry title was then legendary because of Vauxhall's success in the 1910 Prince Henry of Prussia Tour, Martin began seeking another which would stamp his car with an equal record of success. 'All the best and most attractive names seemed to have been taken', Lionel Martin wrote in *Motor Sport*, November, 1944. 'After reviewing all the flowers, beasts, birds and fishes that we knew, we got to place-names, and as my Singer had recently scored a point or two at the Hertfordshire County AC's Aston Clinton hill-climb, the first part of that name was adopted with acclamation, and my humble cognomen appended to it.'

So far as Vauxhall was concerned, the Twenty was not the only model to gain any success at Aston Clinton. Pomeroy's other great car, the 30/98, was a Shelsley Walsh record-holder; indeed, it scored 75 'firsts' between 1920 and 1923 in hill-climb and track events, including Shelsley Walsh and Brooklands. And so far as names are concerned Vauxhall have usually played on the alliteration of the 'V', with Velox, Victor, Ventora and Viva, or with the 'C's' such as Cadet and Cresta.

As so many types were produced in the early years, the main theme of the Vauxhall story will be easier to understand if basic facts are given of models following the successful 20 hp.

The 12/16 in its 20·9 hp form ceased production in 1908 (that is the car already mentioned as being the first live-axle, not chain-driven Vauxhall), and Pomeroy's 20 hp continued in production for five years. The '27' of 1909 lasted for only one year in the Luton list. This was a six-cylinder 26·8 hp car costing £535 for chassis only, and a smaller 17·9 four-cylinder model was introduced at the same, equally short-lived. There was a 16 hp car known as a 'semi-racer' but very different from racers of today. Basically it was a two-seater with a minute dickey (rumble) seat. The year 1910 saw the introduc-

Above. Prototype of the famous Prince Henry C-type, its designer Lawrence Pomeroy at the wheel. This is at Lynmouth, Devon, after prolonged testing in 1912.
Below. Raymond Mays' Vauxhall-Villiers, taking just over 45·5 sec. at a Shelsley Walsh hill-climb in July, 1929. Supercharged model was developed by Amherst Villiers from the 1922 TT car.

Above HM King George V arrives at Vimy Ridge in a Vauxhall, 1917, 'as far as a car could go'.
Below. HRH Prince Philip, Duke of Edinburgh, inspects a 1905 model at the RAC Golden Jubilee celebrations. This model differs from that shown on the frontispiece of this book by having a 9 hp three-cylinder engine, wheel steering, and artillery wheels.

Above. The Vauxhall board-room, built in 1905 when the move to Luton was made, and in use exactly like this today. In 1905 about 100 cars a year were made; today over 350,000.
Below. Luton machine-shop, 1920.

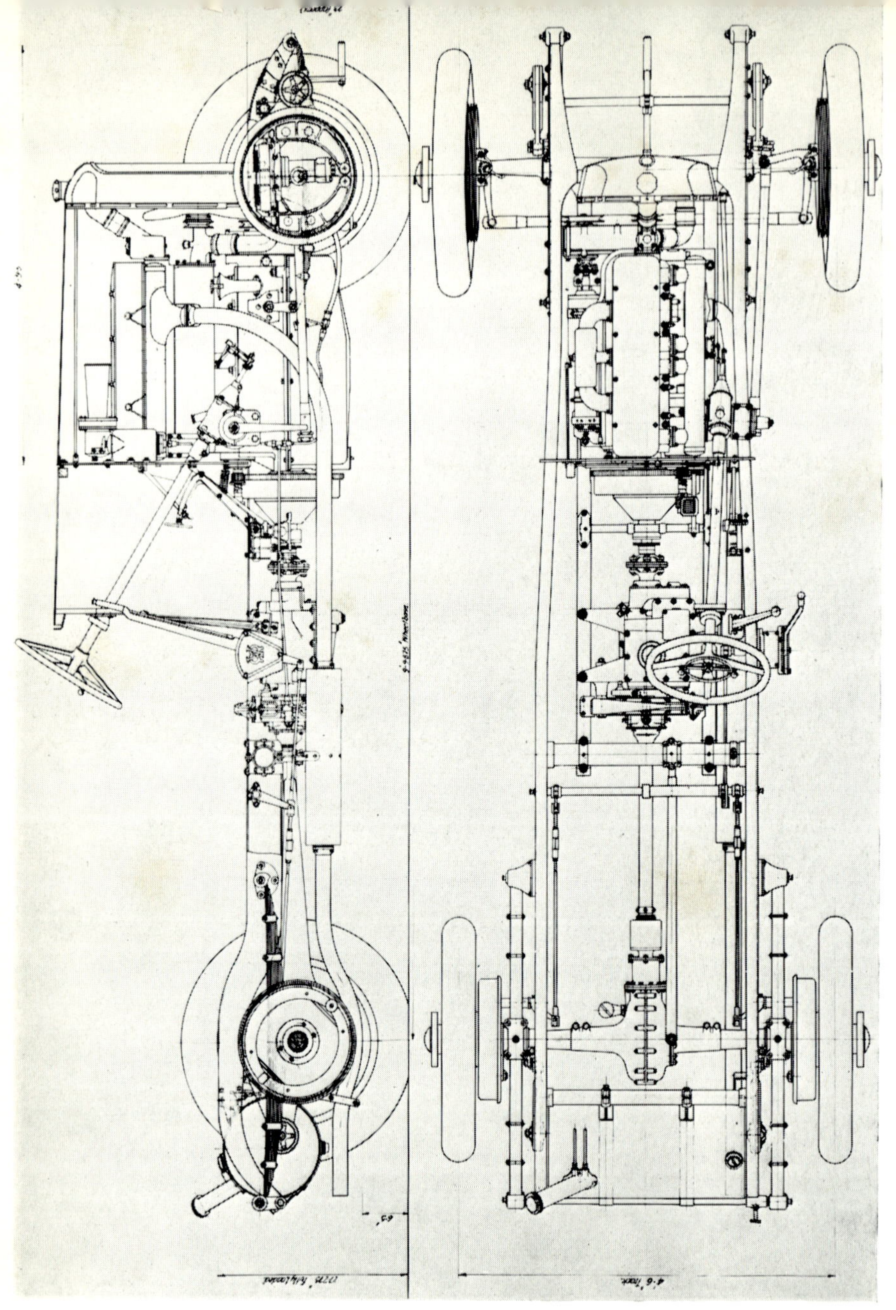

Chassis diagrams of the classic 30/98 OE-type.

tion of the '30' and the forerunner of Pomeroy's Prince Henry C-type. The standard '30' continued in production until 1912. It had a six-cylinder engine, with the ubiquitous internal dimensions of 90 × 120 mm, 880 × 120 tyres, 11 ft. 3 in. wheelbase, all told a costly chassis in 1910 at £605 (then about $1,400). To avoid confusion, it must be recorded here that the Prince Henry was a four-cylinder model, produced first to the standard bore/stroke dimensions of 90 × 120, increased later to 95 × 140 mm to give a 22·5 hp unit. There are examples of several of these early cars, including the 'semi-racer' and the Prince Henry in the Vauxhall Motors' collection.

Not all development was along these lines. In 1912, for instance, one might come across the six-cylinder 35 hp cabriolet on the B–12 chassis. One such was built for the Russian royal family, who had a distinct preference for Vauxhall cars at this period, when the Company maintained a workshop in Russia, staffed by engineers from Britain. There was even a lavish catalogue of Vauxhall models printed in Russian.

In 1913 came the most famous Vauxhall of all pre-GM years, the so-called '30/98', which is dealt with in a later chapter of this book. But it may be noted here that the rather inaccurate 30/98 label was given *after* the car had been accepted by the sporting public (in its day the Prince Henry was known as a fast light touring car, not a sports car), and the Luton label for the 30/98 initially was the Velox, a name introduced for the first time. Owing to the sporting successes of Vauxhall in the Dominions, two special 'Colonial' 20 hp models had been introduced; while these might now be written off lightly as past history, the interesting fact is that one of these 20 hp chassis was equipped with a two-seater body and a goods platform at the back—not exactly a Bedford, but Vauxhall's first estate car or practical pick-up. These 'Colonials' had larger wheels and different gear-ratios from the home products.

During the First World War Luton built nearly 2,000 cars for the War Office, and naturally these saw hard service in many countries. Looking through the historic Luton records (some of the photographs are reproduced in this present book) one sees, for example, a 25 hp Vauxhall staff car carrying General Allenby on his victor's entry into Jerusalem. Another Vauxhall took King George V to Vimy Ridge across Flanders mud. Yet another '25' staff car made two trips from Salonika to Santa Quaranta on the Adriatic, over four mountain ranges in Greece and Albania. Another '25' was the first car to cross the Rhine into Germany after the 1918 Armistice. Between 1914 and 1920 only this 25 hp model was produced, and its war record can perhaps be equalled only by that of the Rolls-Royce Silver Ghost; they point out with pride at Luton how many more '25's' were in service, and in how many more countries they were driven by the military. In Cairo before the Armistice the Australian driver of a '25' challenged a British officer who claimed to have the fastest car in Egypt, a non-British 35 hp vehicle. Over a three-mile run from a standing start the Vauxhall won in 3 min. 2·25 sec., being 13·5 sec. faster than its bigger opponent.

In 1921, and in production for five years, came the 14/40, a four-cylinder (75 × 130) car costing £650 complete with body; but there was a major change the following year when the '23/60' was introduced, developed from the wartime '25', It was Vauxhall's first overhead-valve engine, and shared some of the components of the 30/98 which was also in time given an ohv engine. We were now in a period of post-war inflation, and the 23/60 available in several open tourer or saloon (sedan) forms carried an average price ticket of £895. The stripped chassis was available at £695, but so smart was the standard Vauxhall coachwork that it is doubtful if more than a few chassis were sold to outside coachbuilders.

Longevity and high craftsmanship were features of these Vauxhalls, starting the quality tradition. As proof I was present at Luton in December, 1969, when a 14/40 Princeton tourer was handed over to Mr. E. Wooderson to join the Vauxhall collection of historic cars. It was driven in by Tom Gibson, grandson of the original owner. The car had been in service with the same Devon family since 1923.

And now—1925, the year in which Vauxhall Motors became part of General Motors Corporation. On the production lines were the 30/98, the 14/40, and the 23/60. A very superior Vauxhall limousine listed as the 25/70 was produced in small numbers between 1925 and 1927. Few today recall it, any more than they realise the Company was also investigating the motor-cycle market in the 1920's when some prototype four-cylinder machines were built, but considered not commercially viable. However, with the 25/70, Vauxhall were making a serious bid for the top-luxury market, and the single-sleeve-valve engine was a most interesting engineering experiment. The 24·7 hp engine had 81·5 × 124 mm dimensions, large-section 33 × 6·75's were fitted, and the catalogue listed some quite exotic coachwork designs at costs ranging between £1,350 and £1,675, depending on specification. For another £250 or so one could purchase a Rolls-Royce Phantom II, also introduced in 1925. That Vauxhall could compete at all in this sphere is in part due to Vauxhall's fine war record and to early international sporting successes.

Consider what a shield of honour this was.

In 1908 there were, all told, successes in three trials and four hill-climbs, and the following year Kidner and Pomeroy saw their cars gaining first prizes and special awards in 13 track events, six hill-climbs and three reliability trials. By 1913 the Pomeroy influence on Vauxhall's sports programme was showing (although this term was then unknown), and similar results were obtained in 35 hill-climbs, 23 track events and 14 reliability trials. The Vauxhall team led by P. C. Kidner was responsible for a large proportion of these successes. There were by now many private Vauxhall owners competing as well. Amateur drivers sometimes identified themselves with a company, and in the 1912 French Grand Prix a team of three specially-built 15·9 hp cars were entered and driven by A. J. Hancock and W. Watson as the company's drivers, and by Percy Lambert as an amateur.

Darbyshire records that three cars were entered for Vauxhall in the 1909 Irish Trials. Of these, one was driven by Hancock and one by F. W. Hodges, both cars being '20's'. The third was a 24 hp car, a prototype not then on the market, driven by Percy Kidner. Another 20 hp was entered privately. The course ran from Dublin to Port Rush, Bundoran, Killarney and back to Dublin. Regulations were very strict, and not only were competitors and cars weighed, but overcoats and 'other wraps' taken into consideration. For this sort of reason one of the Vauxhall team failed to comply with regulations and was disqualified at the end of the trial after distinguishing himself on hill-climbs. The others were first and second in their class. Hancock's Vauxhall received a gold medal and obtained 995·13 marks put of 1,000, two marks being lost because there was slight play in a front bearing at the end of the course. The Scottish Trials took place over six days in June, 10 days after the return from Ireland. Kidner's and Hancock's 20's were worked on day and night to get them ready again, and once more there was a confusing weight regulation. This involved carrying a 'lead passenger' of 160 lb. Hancock reported that: 'He was very quiet and gave no trouble at all.'

Both the 20's were successful in their classes. Kidner had one stop for tyres, but was fastest on all hills except one where he was baulked by a straying spectator. Hancock made a non-stop run throughout, returning fastest times on four hills.

And now Brooklands, where Vauxhall began to make its mark. The first driver to score a Brooklands win was one Seltz, at that time a Vauxhall director, in the Whit Saturday and Monday meeting of 1909. The speeds were not startling (there are complete details in Boddy's classic history of Brooklands), but he nevertheless managed to gain three firsts, two seconds and three thirds, which, all in all, was not a bad debut for Vauxhall on the track. Then, in August, Kidner and Hancock took first and second places in the O'Gorman event at Brooklands, with standard 20 hp cars stripped of all bodywork. Successes at Shelsley followed that same year, Hancock winning the President's Cup (Vauxhall's second successive victory here), and Kidner the Henry Edmunds Trophy. Both cars were those which had completed the Irish and Scottish Trials.

Is racing worth while? That question is always being asked, and doubted by executives of firms who draw out from the track. But, as Darbyshire points out, it is interesting to note the development of engine power which took place around that time when Vauxhall were so successful on hills, in trials and on the track. Between March and July, 1909, when it was tuned for Shelsley, the 20 hp engine of Hancock's Vauxhall showed an increase in power from 39 to 52·6 hp, at 2,370 rpm.

Vauxhall enthusiasts will frequently have noted a disc-wheel, torpedo-like single-seater car of the 1909 era, with the initials KN on the nose; photographs of it appear in almost every museum and Vauxhall biography. It is Hancock's hotted 20 hp in record-breaking trim. The 'KN' is an indication that it was hot stuff, a sample of early-twentieth-century humour. Its first success was on 14th December, 1909, when with Hancock at the wheel it established a record for the flying half-mile at 88·6 mph. He also covered ten laps at 81.33 mph to capture the long record, and although a 20 hp the speed recorded was actually better than that at Brooklands for the 40 hp category.

The year 1910 was mainly notable for the extremely good showing of the Vauxhall team of three in the Prince Henry of Prussia tour. Prince Henry, a very keen motorist who took part in the event, intended that it should be a thorough test for standard touring cars, and the tour of some 1,200 miles included speed trials at two points. We shall look closer at the

Prince Henry in Chapter 5, but at this point the story of the 20 hp is far from complete. In October, 1910, the magic 'ton' was obtained by Hancock at the wheel of his 20 hp in yet another guise. Many manufacturers throughout the world were making strenuous attempts to be the first to achieve three figures in the 21 hp class, and as Vauxhall held the long and short records for this rating they were naturally more than anxious not to lose their leading place.

Three attempts had to be made in the October before the magic hundred came up. On 7th October Hancock managed 97·15, and a fortnight later after timing adjustments had been made a speed of 98·1 mph was clocked. Finally on 26th October the flying half-mile was completed at 100·08, and although this may not seem very much today on a foreign motorway where such speeds are possible, if not legal, it was a very different story back in 1910. In addition to the speed record, the Vauxhall list of successes for that year includes 10 first, four second and seven third prizes; and for the second year running the first two places in the O'Gorman Trophy fell to Vauxhalls. Firsts at Rivington Pike again, gold cups at Shelsley, the Somerset AC Hill-climb and other events were becoming almost routine.

Of course it was impossible to foresee the dramatic change to come in Russian social life within a decade, and in 1911 Luton was gratified that Kidner and his team chalked up an international success in the Russian Reliability Trials, in which, of course, most other leading Continental luxury cars were represented—all with an eye to their manufacturers establishing themselves in Russian cities. In September Percy Kidner drove a standard 20 hp from St Petersburg (Leningrad) to Sevastopol without loss of a single mark.

Then came a Luton attack on the 16 hp class records, an interesting development, since at that time all the Vauxhall racing cars, whether owned privately or by the Company, were 20's. However, there was a fine challenge from Lion

Peugeot, which up to that time had not been beaten in the '16' class. While some 16 hp and 12/16 Vauxhalls were still being sold in the standard ranges, the racing model was in no way standard. This was the heyday of the long-stroke engine, and with the racing 16 the decision was taken to have a bore of 80 mm and a stroke of 200! This resulted in the cylinder head having to project through the bonnet cowling, which was unfortunate since, judged by contemporary aircraft standards these bodies with their 'faired-in' bodies were well streamlined.

This ungainly-looking record-breaker was successful up to a point. On 4th November it raised the half-mile record in this 16 hp class from 90·04 mph (Peugeot) to 97·67, and 10 laps from a standing start were covered at 91·46 mph, nearly a 10 mph increase over the Lion Peugeot. Unfortunately they tried to push it too hard, to get the magic 'ton' over the flying half-mile, resulting in a broken big-end and the emergence of a piston through the sump.

The success pattern of track racing continued throughout 1912 (including the O'Gorman Trophy for the third time), and in that November Hancock's 20 hp gained the world record for 50 miles in 30 mins. 52 secs. at an average speed of 97·15 mph. In achieving this he also took the 21 hp class record for the flying half-mile at 101·24 mph and sundry other records, and two days later he succeeded in establishing a new record for the kilometre at 101·403 mph.

In that year no official Vauxhall drivers took part in the 2,000-mile Russian Trials from St Petersburg to Moscow, but a 20 hp was privately entered by a Russian motorist who won prizes for speed events at Riga and Warsaw in the course of the Trials, and for a hill-climb at Kiev.

Extraordinary happenings marred Vauxhall's entry in the Swedish Trials which took place in the February. The weather was most severe—at times 40°F below zero—and Percy Kidner, who wore only an ordinary English motoring coat, countered the weather with a canvas protective hood to the dashboard, raised to eye-level so that snow which fell into the slipstream passed over his head. The floorboard was drilled so heat could rise under this canvas cover from the engine. Protected in this way, Kidner had an advantage over other drivers, many of whom suffered badly from frostbite. Unfortunately he forged ahead too fast, arrived home one and a half hours before the next car and, according to the regulations, being too far ahead to receive an award. All the same, Kidner and the Vauxhall were given a victor's reception on arrival in Stockholm.

The year 1913 was probably the most successful in the sporting world Vauxhalls ever enjoyed, and this was undoubtedly due in large measure to the appearance of the 30/98. As we shall see in the next chapter, it was neither a 30 nor a 98, and for track events it was always entered at its RAC rating of 23·8 hp. Its first success came at Waddington Fells the day after the first model was delivered to Lancashire. Fastest-time and other successes came at Shelsley, Aston, Caerphilly and Saltburn, besides several Brooklands successes at the mid-summer and August meetings.

This advent of the 30/98 overshadows all other sporting successes of the year. It was a car which would lap Brooklands comfortably at over the 100, and many were the battles between Vauxhall and such famous racing marques as Talbot and Sunbeam.

More Russian successes followed, with racing sometimes taking place on frozen lakes. There was the occasion of a race over the Gulf of Riga, frozen and in heavy snow, when out of 11 starters only five cars finished. Two Vauxhalls were placed first and fourth respectively. It is interesting to record that now, in the Seventies, ice-racing is a popular Scandinavian sport, the Viva GT is pre-eminent, and currently Bo Bostra is the champion.

In that fateful August of 1913 when rumours of a possible 'Kaiser war' were already rife, and the storm was to burst over Europe within the twelvemonth, Hancock set out to attack the 12-hour record. Unfortunately there was a rare early-morning August fog, and the 12-hour attempt had to be abandoned, since it would ultimately have involved driving in darkness. Frustrated and angry, Hancock nevertheless drove through the day to break records nearly every hour. His Vauxhall took all the 100-mile records from 300 to 700, at varying speeds ranging between 87·74 to 92·11 mph. In the course of this he smashed all hour records from four to nine.

Luck must have been with Hancock that day because, as a dramatic event proved, the 12-hour record would never have been taken.

Shortly after taking the 700-mile record, when 80 miles ahead of the previous holder, the Vauxhall was seen to be in difficulties on the Brooklands banking. A reporter of *The Autocar* said: 'Hancock swung under the Member's bridge high on the banking at a terrific speed, the car bounding and jerking as it took the bumps on the curve. Then, as it passed over the bridge spanning the River Wey, the driver seemed suddenly to be in trouble.

'He was clutching at the wheel, and the spectators could see his hands move up and down. . . . Then, to the horror of all, the car instead of cutting down, seemed to shoot up and run right to the top of the banking. A cloud of dust spurted up as the wheels took the edge, and then—it swayed on down the slope . . . Hancock made a mighty effort and just slewed the almost uncontrollable car round past the time-keepers at the bottom of the slope, missing them and the indicator by inches. . . .'

A lug of the offside spring hanger had broken as the result of the terrific hammering at high speed, so the spring was held on only at the back. Hancock's superb skill and coolness avoided what could otherwise have been a major disaster.

E

5

Prince Henry and the 30/98

Whenever the 'greats' of byegone days are talked about—I mean cars such as the Rolls-Royce Silver Ghost, the early Benz and Mercs, Austro-Daimlers and the rest—the Prince Henry is certain to be mentioned.

In one important sense the comparison is not apt, since there were several versions of this classic car, first put on the market in the year 1911 as a 20 hp fast light tourer, and even in their day open tourers were sometimes described as Prince Henry's—both the 20 and 25 hp models—when, in fact, they were nothing of the sort.

The story of the Prince Henry development goes back to the first years of Laurence H. Pomeroy at Luton, when he joined as an assistant draughtsman. Nobody then could foresee the day when he would be designing cars destined to make the name Vauxhall famous all over Europe. Nobody, moreover, could foresee what would happen when Pomeroy, as a schoolboy, failed his matriculation exam (akin to present-day 'A'-levels) because of his low marks in French. What possible connection could this have with designing a fast car that would take the French Peugeot and others by the ears?

The answer is that, at 24, Pomeroy was a Whitworth Exhibitioner but still smarting from having failed matric, so in his spare time he began a do-it-yourself course to improve his French using books in a subject, engineering, with which he was familiar. By a lucky chance he found a copy of a text book by Heirman, in the French language, entitled *L'Automobile à l'Essence: Principes des Construction at Calcul* ('The

Petrol-engined Car'). For its day it was a forward-looking textbook. Written in an era when the slow-running petrol engine was not very different from the gas engine, it dealt with the problems of increasing power output by higher compression ratios, and getting improved performance by larger port and valve-opening areas. What *L'Automobile à l'Essence* did to Pomeroy's familiarity with French verbs is now unimportant; what matters is that it opened for him the way to a practical new philosophy—the development of a fast touring engine with extremely large valves, lighter reciprocating parts and higher compression ratio. The Vauxhall 3-litre engine was developing around 23–25 bhp at 1,800 rpm, and Pomeroy astounded his technical colleagues at Luton when he expressed his belief this output could be increased to 40 bhp, and that the maximum rpm rate could safely be increased. Precisely what this engine could do in a suitable chassis we have seen in Chapter 4, and the final car was dubbed the 'Prince Henry' after the fine performance of the Vauxhall threesome in the Prince Henry of Prussia Tour, in competition with Benz, NSU, Rolls-Royce and others.

There can be little harm now in disclosing that Pomeroy was taking something of a gamble in entering the car for the original Trials, since although the revs had been pushed up to 2,400, and the compression ratio increased to give a 38 bhp output, this was not completely the anticipated power. Worse, the engine tended to pre-ignite after about five minutes of full-throttle bench-testing. However, it was believed that on the road in a reliability trial such as the RAC 2,000 Miles, it would not be possible to run full throttle for such a length of time. As is now a matter of motoring history, the 20 hp in this form was 37 seconds faster on major hills than any others in its class.

The late Laurence R. Pomeroy, son of the Prince Henry designer, was a familiar figure to devotees of veteran and vintage cars for many years, as he appeared at many major events at the wheel of his beautifully preserved Prince Henry Vauxhall. At various times Laurence and I were with the (then) Temple Press, publishers of *The Motor*, and for this company Pom was producing his book *The Mini Story* at the time I was finalising the proofs of my own *The Book of the Mini*. This was also the occasion of my first visit to Detroit and to the main centre of General Motors, so whenever Pom and I met we had high-spirited discussions about the relative merits of the 'new' and 'old' Vauxhalls. On learning that I was researching for a book on Vauxhall, he gave me some of his memoirs about the Prince Henry and his father's development work on it, and these notes he also used for an article about the historic car which he wrote for *The Vintage and Veteran Magazine*.

LHP—as Pom invariably referred to his father—was restricted in the equipment he was able to use for the first special 20 hp chassis, so most of the new design and practice first went into the power unit. Those were the days of splash lubrication. LHP provided full pressure lubrication to help cool bearings of an engine running faster and under greater stress from a higher compression ratio. A five-bearing crankshaft was used right from the start, and this was machined lighter than others in engines of the same power output.

The first chassis had a cone clutch driving a four-speed box, which LHP, like Royce, believed to be essential for success in hill-climbing and other competition work. There was no four-speed box available at the time (although there was such a box on the 18 hp car of 1907), so one was converted from a three-speed box. The layshaft was altered, and the problem of incorporating reverse involved having a separate lever for a supplementary reverse gear. There was an open propeller shaft to the rear axle, and a well-thought-out torque-arm arrangement at the back.

Soon the cone clutch was abandoned in favour of a multi-plate assembly, to transmit the higher power coming from subsequent 60 bhp engines; Pomeroy pointed out to me a charming phrase from the 1912 Prince Henry instruction book: 'If the clutch is working well, i.e. so that a top speed along the level can be accomplished with ease . . .' The makeshift gearbox was soon abandoned, and the Pomeroy-designed four-speed box which replaced it remained virtually unchanged throughout the rest of the Prince Henry's long life.

In the preceding chapter we saw how trials successes were being gained, and that the 20 hp class records were shattered by a chassis on which was mounted a cigar-like narrow single seater body. With Hancock at the wheel it covered the flying half-mile at 88·6 mph. In 1910 this same design of side-valve engine had been developed to 60 bhp, and this was the version A. J. Hancock used for the Brooklands 100 mph attempt. Incidentally, a contemporary record discloses that Pomeroy and the Brooklands team were bitterly disappointed by the 98·1 mph attained on 22nd October, since at that point little more could be done with the carburation or timing. It was suggested that oil-drag was cutting the speed by two or three miles an hour, so the gearbox and axle were drained, and that is how the magic 100·8 mph came up.

'In this year also', said Laurence Pomeroy, 'it was decided to enter the 1910 Prince Henry Trials in Germany, and LHP's note books show that he planned an original and elaborate power unit for this. . . . It was to have an overhead camshaft with double the number of cams, so that it could be moved endwise to give one valve-timing for maximum torque at low speeds and another for high power output at around 2,800 rpm. The inclined valves were of abnormal size, and this proved its undoing, for the gas velocity was so low that it failed to equal the power given by developed versions of the 1908 side-valve engine. . . .'

The team of three cars prepared for the Prince Henry Trials therefore used the basic production side-valve engine. They had the characteristic high-sided and doorless bodies, with the new V-fronted radiator with flutes running into grooves continuing for the full length of the bonnet. This was a more sporting development of the parallel flutes introduced earlier.

In competition against the huge 7-litre engines of Benz, Austro-Daimler and other entries, the Vauxhalls made a fine showing but obviously could not sweep the board. Because of the 'Prince Henry' title later given to the type, it is sometimes wrongly assumed they were the overall victors, which was not the case. The Trial was won by Dr. Porsche, driving an Austro-Daimler which he had designed. However, the Vauxhalls were completely reliable, which is more than could be said for some other Continental entries, and the timed speeds achieved of just over 70 mph on bad road surfaces were astoundingly good for a touring four-seater. This European acclaim, coupled with the O'Gorman event success and the record-breaking at Brooklands, unified the other Vauxhall directors behind their chief engineer. As Pomeroy said of LHP's work following the German Trials: 'The directors became completely satisfied that the high-output engine running at the remarkably high speed of 2,500 rpm could safely be put in the hands of the public, and it was against this background that the Prince Henry sporting four-seater was displayed at the Motor Show.

'During 1912 some 50 cars of this type (that is, with the 80 × 120 mm engine installed in the 9 ft. 6 in. wheelbase chassis, 4 ft. 6 in. track) were made, and in the hands of their owners began to compete with immense success in hill-climbs and competitions of every kind.

'The life of the 3-litre was, however, brief, and during 1912 the same chassis was fitted with a 4-litre 95 × 140 mm engine. This had been introduced in the first place for the 25 hp touring car which had a 10 ft. 10 in. wheelbase chassis, and 4 ft. 8 in. track. Although weighing only 500 lb, this new engine developed 75 bhp, about 20 bhp more than the production-type 3-litres, and this naturally put up the performance. . . . Unfortunately the 3-litre radiator had insufficient cooling area, and this model was notorious for boiling if driven fast upon a summer's day. . . . Nevertheless, this small, light car was tremendous fun to drive, and I remember as a boy many long journeys sitting in the dickey-seat of my father's two seater.'

By 1913 the larger engine was fitted in the 10 ft. 10 in. chassis. Bigger four-seater bodies could now be fitted, and this is really when the Prince Henry type became accepted as a high-speed tourer rather than as a light sports model.

How does the Prince Henry relate to the 30/98? In his notes describing the enlarged 4-litre unit, Laurence Pomeroy said: 'This was in August, 1913, and already the 30/98 was in being. This model was to become Vauxhall's major contribution to sports-car design, but it should be remembered that the engine was in fact a bored-out Prince Henry (from 95 to 98 mm), with the 70 mm (cold) throw crankshaft stretched to 75 mm. This gave a $4\frac{1}{2}$-litre swept volume. This enlarged engine was put into the original small Prince Henry chassis, so that strictly speaking the E-type, as it was called, was a straightforward development of the C-type Prince Henry.

'But whereas only a few 30/98's were built before the outbreak of the First World War in August 1914 the Company made a hundred of the short-wheelbase cars with a 4-litre engine, and 200 of the "big" Prince Henry.'

The Autocar of the time remarked that it was a wonderful car and delightful to drive, then went on to comment: 'There was no opportunity for testing the top limit of speed, but from the slowest crawl to 50 mph or more there is scarcely any perceptible change in quietness or smoothness. When one knows by speedometer that the engine is revolving at 2,000 rpm at least, it is difficult to believe that such really is the case. Not only is the car, as a whole, smooth as well as highly efficient in the usual sense of the term, but it is even smoother than many cars for which no suggestion of high power-output or unusual efficiency is made.'

There are several surviving examples of the Prince Henry

Vauxhalls in Britain today to remind us of the era of the Prince Henry and Herkomer Trials, although in fact these are 4-litre cars developed from the experienced gained in Europe. The limitations of the Prince Henry were only those of the era, and the road-holding was very good considering the high bodywork and relatively narrow track. Performance on the road was restricted by rear-wheel brakes and a transmission brake, but, of course, this was standard practice for most high-grade cars of the period. The long half-elliptics 'cart' springs gave good road-holding, and with solid axles it was possible to get a Prince Henry round corners faster than can be done with some modern sports cars.

In its final development the Prince Henry had the bored-out 3,969 cc engine (95 × 140 mm), magneto high-tension ignition, 12-volt electric lighting, Hele-Shaw multi-plate clutch driving the Pomeroy-designed four-speed gearbox, and open shaft drive to rear axle.

Nowadays when so many great companies have withdrawn from sponsoring entries in sporting events, the question has to be faced as to whether the Prince Henry was *worth while*, from the point of view of the relatively small Luton concern. The car had made the name Vauxhall famous on the Continent, and world records were smashed. Laurence Pomeroy looked at the achievement this way: 'It must be emphasised,' he told me, 'that these results were attained by completely orthodox means, the design being not only efficient but also simple, and —not less important—profitable. Between 1908 and 1914 Vauxhall built fewer than 2,000 cars, at prices varying (in terms of modern money) between £1,000 and £2,500, for an overall profit of little less than a quarter of a million pounds. This combination of giving pleasure to the buyer and profit to the producer must be rare indeed.'

To summarise, the first V-radiator Prince Henry cars appeared in 1910, one was shown at the 1911 Motor Show, and they went into production the following year. The larger car with the 4-litre engine was the D-type, and a variant was the D-type engine in the original short A-type chassis. There is some confusion in referring to early Vauxhall records, since (as Laurence Pomeroy confirmed) the works also retained a special hill-climb car which was basically a 1912 *Coupé de l'Auto* team car, with a short-tailed two-seater body.

At that time Vauxhalls were approached by Mr. Joseph Higginson, a noted automobile engineer and well-to-do North-country sportsman, remembered today not only for the part he played in instigating the 30/98 formula but as the inventor of the Autovac vacuum fuel-feed system adopted internationally by dozens of manufacturers in the 1920's. Up to 1912 he made a name for himself in competitions with his 80 hp La Buire, and he was anxious to obtain a British-built car with an even better performance on hills, particularly Shelsley Walsh. The record then was held by H. C. Holder's 58 hp Daimler, with a time of 62·2 secs. Sunbeam and Talbot competition induced Higginson to approach a number of British manufacturers.

Unfortunately his suggestion did not reach Pomeroy until March, 1913, and he needed a car for the June Shelsley meeting. Doubtless he believed something suitable might be on the stocks, but after discussions about the Prince Henry, Pomeroy assured his client the Company would be willing to provide a special car to his specification within little more than twelve weeks—using the Prince Henry as a basis. A record of those days was kept by Mr. George Sanders, noted owner of E and OE-type 30/98's, and the following account is based on his notes.

This very first Higginson car had a 4,526 cc engine (98 × 150 mm), and similar five-bearing crankshaft and valve layout as on the Prince Henry. There were high-lift cams. Various axle ratios were experimented with. An all-aluminium narrow body without doors was designed, and to overcome the boiling problems associated with the earlier V-front radiator, Pomeroy provided a flat-fronted radiator, fluted, with a more powerful imposing appearance than the Prince Henry, the production models of which continued to be fitted with the projecting-V style of radiator.

Pomeroy's Luton crew worked at breakneck speed to finish this special model for Higginson, who wanted to enter it for a few events near his home before having a crack at Shelsley Walsh in June. In fact the car was ready in time for him to attack Rivington Pike, in the Lancashire AC's May meeting, at which he chalked up fastest time of day. Similar success came a week or two later, on the Aston hill.

Shelsley at that time had an atrocious surface, and many cars failed to complete the 1,133-yard hill, let alone show a reasonable time. Such was the nature of the climb with its difficult double bends, that even 20 or 30 mph could produce spectacular motoring. On his first run with the new car Higginson clocked 70 sec. as he accustomed himself to handling something so much lighter than his La Buire. On the second run he clocked 58 sec., which was quite remarkable. One of the new racing Sunbeams then made a better time, while Higginson and his friends decided the Vauxhall might do better if it had more weight at the back for adhesion. In this they were perfectly correct.

On the next run he took three passengers, and the ugly 1,133 yards with their middle double bends were covered at an average of 42 mph, recording the remarkable time of only 55·2 sec. Not only did this beat Higginson's own previous best time on the heavy La Buire by about 13 sec., but it was a record to stand for 15 years.

Pomeroy's works version of the car clocked up Brooklands successes, as we have already seen, and Higginson continued to produce a string of competition and hill-climb successes. The two cars jointly secured 13 first and second places in major events. Bertelli also scored success at the wheel of a 30/98, and in May, 1914, it took second place in the Russian Grand Prix, at an average speed of 70·8 mph over a killing circuit. In all only five 30/98's were built in 1913, seven in 1914, one in 1915, then no more until 1919. The original cost was £1,960, and the model did not really get into production until postwar years.

During the First World War the fast light touring 30/98 was somewhat overshadowed by the rugged '25' and it was nearly two years after the war that the next series of E-types was in production. As has already been said, the '30/98' label was a misnomer, probably deliberately so. These figures would convey to the sporting motorist the fact that the engine had an RAC-formula rating of 30 bhp (a pardonable exaggeration), and a maximum output of 98 hp. In fact the RAC rating was 23·8, and the '98' may have been chosen as a retort to another internationally famed car, the Mercedes 38/90.

When production started after the war Luton made a determined bid for the new sporting market and marketed it with a touring body then known as the Velox at a reduced figure of only £1,676. Those were the days! The depression in industry prevented many prices from rising, and by 1924 the Velox was cut to £1,220. In some respects they were austerity times, and it was afterwards rumoured that Vauxhall were able to reduce the price of the 30/98 by some determined bargaining for low-cost accessories. The first electric-lighting system was certainly not of the best and there were rumours that Luton had managed to make a small saving in carburation costs by buying up ex-Air Ministry aircraft carburetters at two shillings each. The usual carburetter found nowadays on a 30/98 is the type RA Zenith, fed, of course, from one of Mr. Higginson's Autovacs.

Through the years, Bentley, Bugatti, Lagonda and other enthusiasts have derided the 30/98's brakes, which at first were modelled on the Prince Henry pattern. The transmission brake could skid the car completely around if mis-applied, but as there were no front brakes the overall braking effort was insufficient for the 30/98's performance. Late in 1923 a front brake system was introduced, and a few of the final-series cars were fitted with an hydraulic system. Braking was never a completely satisfactory feature of the 30/98, which perhaps did not matter overmuch in an age when cars were made to go fast, and stopping was a secondary consideration. One critic of this Vauxhall model said the only way to get out of trouble on a 30/98 was to steer, change down, jump out or pray—preferably in that order!

The original Velox bodywork was modified through the years, by 1927 the wings were redesigned along Bentley lines, and the whole car became more generally acceptable judged by modern views of what motoring in the '20's ought to have been. Like it or not, the 20's were the heyday of the boat-type body, and the boat-backed 2/3-seater Wensom body was introduced on the 30/98 in 1926. This odd name is not an inversion of Newsom, as some supposed, but merely the name of a Norfolk river where A. J. Hancock enjoyed some fast boating.

Pomeroy had plans for an overhead-cam Prince Henry engine, but this was not put into production; in fact LHP had left Luton nearly two years before his successor C. E. King decided to take the obvious step of redesigning the engine for a fairly conventional push-rod ohv arrangement.

This gave the car greater flexibility, and was in line with the engineering philosophy of the time. The side-valve E-type peaked at around 2,800 rpm, but the overhead-valve engine was designed for a maximum of 3,500 rpm, at which it produced 112 bhp. This OE-type had a shorter stroke, 140 mm instead of 150, which reduced the capacity slightly to 4,224 cc from 4,526 cc. The earlier engine pulled a 2·5-to-1 top, reduced to 3-to-1 for most production E-types: with the faster-revving ohv engine the gearing was altered to give a 3.3-to-1 top.

That great vintage-car personality Tim Carson, secretary of the Vintage Sports-Car Club and a mine of information on early Vauxhalls, had said of the E-type in general and of a car of which he was particularly fond: 'One of the chief charms of the car is its ability to pull away smoothly from 8 to 10 mph in top gear, and to accelerate smartly in the upper seventies with no fuss. The maximum is in the region of 80 mph, but when in first-class order the 30/98 was capable of 85 mph or more in touring trim, and of over 100 mph when stripped at Brooklands. The body and wings are aluminium, and the german-silver radiator and copper pipes for water, oil and petrol repay the work of polishing, for the engine when nicely kept is a pleasure to see, reminding one rather of a marine engine.'

The E-type showed engine revs of 1,000 rpm at 33 mph, but life was different with the ohv version. As Tim said: 'With the new engine higher speeds were possible, over 120 mph being recorded at Brooklands by specially tuned cars, but the axle ratio was altered to 3·3 to 1, and some of the flexibility and low-speed torque were lost. Owners of the E-type tend to consider the OE models as "Buzz-boxes", as they barely do 30 mph at a thousand revolutions a minute!'

By comparison, a present-day typical Viva engine has a capacity of 1,159 cc, about one-quarter that of the E-type. Instead of peaking at 3,500 rpm, it runs happily up to 5,400 rpm or more, at which the output is over 56 bhp. The Viva 1600 produces 83 bhp at 5,800. This is not an indication of any poor design in the E-type, or of an amazing development in the 1970's—simply the general progression of power output and smooth torque for a much smaller, lighter engine of 8.5-to-1 compression ratio, made possible by modern alloys, better engine accessories, and improved fuels and lubricants available.

By degrees the E and OE were modified. A direct-drive dynamo was provided by 1924, being an improvement on the earlier CAV dynamos belt-driven from behind the clutch, the wheelbase was lengthened and the ground clearance lowered by two inches, in accordance with current sports-car fashion. Castrol R was specified by Vauxhalls, so most E and OE-types were driven around in a haze of that aromatic lubricant which conjured up visions of Brooklands and Le Mans, until it was found that XL did just as well—and today, of course, GTX does even better in an engine which has been cleaned out to receive it. Very complete maintenance information for all early 30/98's was given in *Motor Sport* of April, 1948, photostat copies of which can be purchased from the Publishing Department of *Motor Sport*, London.

Enthusiastic vintage-car lovers sometimes hear rumours of the OD-type 30/98, and even of an EH-type. There was, indeed, an OD model available in 1924, but not an EH. Stories about it actually refer to an H-type which Pomeroy had intended developing from the original E. It is common knowledge that the E-type was modified to make it into a regular production model during 1914–18, but Laurence R. Pomeroy disclosed in *Motor Sport*: 'It was, however, my father's intention that this car should be regarded as a stop-gap until the manufacturing programme could be rationalised around what was known as the H-type car. This was an overhead-camshaft model of advanced design, the bore and stroke being identical with the 1914 Grand Prix cars, i.e. 100 by 140 mm. The camshaft was driven by eccentrics from the front of the engine, and the cylinder block was deeply spigoted into the light-alloy crankcase. It was intended that this engine should be built with varying degrees of 'tune' to meet the needs of the competition car and the town carriage, and that it should have a rather longer wheelbase than the existing 30/98. On the test-bed it gave some 100 bhp at 2,500 rpm but, following the departure of my father in late 1919 to take up other work in the USA, the directors decided not to go on with the H-type, but to develop the existing engine to use overhead valves operated by push-rods thus converting the E-type into the OE.'

At a time in the mid-'20's when the 30/98 was capturing Vauxhall's share of the sporting market, the 23/60 model (which as we have seen was introduced in 1922) became known as the OD, and was produced alongside the larger 30/98. At the peak of its development, the OD-type had an RAC rating of 22·4, the four-cylinder engine was 95 × 140 mm bore and stroke, and it had a 10 ft. 10 in. wheelbase chassis compared with the OE which in 1924–5 was 9 ft. 10 in. wheelbase. The town-carriage OD had 880 × 120 tyres, or 985 × 135 for limousines, and the chassis weight was about 340 lb heavier than the 30/98. The Carlton limousine and other styles on the OD 22·4 hp chassis did much to enhance Vauxhall's reputation as a high-quality car, and the 30/98 brought added lustre to the *marque* by its sporting successes.

Taking one single year of the 30/98's achievements as typical, consider the 1924 list which excludes racing-car successes, and deals only with distinctions won by standard 30/98's.

The list includes a first place in the 100 mph Short Handicap, BARC (Brooklands) Easter Meeting; *Daily Guardian* (Sydney, Australia), Class C, two Vauxhalls tied for first place in first hill-climb, first and second in flying mile; York & District MC Hill-climb, first; Essex MC Hill-climb, first in classes 71 and 72; Inter-University Hill-climb, first and third; Blackpool Speed Trials, three firsts, two seconds and two thirds; Royal Scottish AC Hill-climb, first: Motor World challenge cup and SMTA prize for fastest time; Vauxhalls made the three fastest times of the day; BARC Midsummer Meeting, one first, one second; Liverpool MC Speed-trials, first, second and third in their class; Shelsley Walsh Hill-climb, second in Class 4 (the TT Vauxhall came first); Boulogne Speed-trials, first in class for 4-litre cars, and first in the sports-car class of the Boulogne Concours d'Elégance. These are the highlights of a busy, successful year.

On the one hand you had Vauxhall's at Luton advertising the 30/98 as: 'The finest sporting car the world produces', and on the other hand there were young men arguing the respective merits of the 30/98 and of the Bentley—arguments which still echo. But what did it all amount to? What was the 30/98's rightful place in the motoring world?

You may get a hint from Beverly R. Kimes' comment in his essay on the 30/98 in *Automobile Quarterly*, Vol. 3, No. 3, when he quotes from Aldous Huxley's novel *Those Barren Leaves*, published in 1925, which was very much a 30/98 vintage year. Kimes reminds us that: 'One of the protagonists of the book was a young milquetoast named Lord Hovenden, who, detached from his motor-car was an entirely different being from the Lord Hovenden who lounged with such deceptive air of languor behind the steering wheel of a Vauxhall Velox. Then he was the most daring and dashing of fellows. It was only when doing 75 mph on the Great North Road that he was able to tell Mrs. Terebinth, 17 years his senior, who had four children and adored her husband, that she was the most beautiful woman he had ever seen. At 80 miles and hour he could tell her he loved her. With the breeze of speed and the sound of the engine to back him up, Lord Hovenden could make all sorts of promises he couldn't keep when his car was in the garage. If only, the hero wished, if only one could spend all one's life in the Vauxhall . . .'

Ah, well, those days have gone, taking with them (except for a few fortunate vintage-car collectors) the sound of a 30/98's burbling exhaust at 33 mph per 1,000 rpm, and also the chance of flirting at 80 mph on the Great North Road.

6

Sir Charles

During the '20's and '30's the engineering prestige of Vauxhall at Luton, born of the 30/98's sporting successes and the craftsmanship of that and later production cars, was high indeed. As this *Vauxhall Companion*, like all other books in the *Companion* series, is part history, part anecdote and part personal reminiscence, there are two facets of those inter-war years which come to my mind and illustrate the double-pronged appeal of Vauxhall in the motoring world.

One memory is of a slight figure clad in black racing leathers, driving to Brooklands in his unique all-weather Silver Ghost, alighting, walking to the pits, then taking a TT Vauxhall out for one of the great Easter or Summer Brooklands meetings, careering around the Byfleet banking at 120 mph, displaying complete mastery of hazards, and doggedly lapping at speeds of around 110 mph. I mean, of course, Jack Barclay the Rolls-Royce 'king'. In 1967 he retired from his Royce and Bentley distributorship in London's Berkeley Square, by then the biggest of its kind in Britain, and concentrated on his 1,000-acre farm. The present generation who knew him only by association with sleek limousines and the JB-1 registration plate seen on his famous Silver Ghost never knew the ex-Royal Flying Corps Jack Barclay of the '20's—a magnificent driver of the kind of fast machinery which in addition to the TT Vauxhall included Austro-Daimler and an enormous Ballot. *Motor Sport*'s Bill Boddy, who has a lifetime of Brooklands records and memories, reminded me of one typical Jack Barclay Vauxhall incident: 'At the 1926 Easter Brooklands Meeting the Vauxhall

F

he was driving was forced up the Byfleet banking and went into a high-speed skid, eventually coming down, turning round, and travelling backwards at some 80 mph. Barclay kept the engine running and continued the race. Later he brought the car out again and won, lapping at nearly 112 mph . . .'

Jack went on to drive a 4½-litre Bentley, and became one of the famous 'Bentley Boys'—joining Woolf Barnato, Dr. J. D. Benjafield, Sir H. R. S. 'Tim' Birkin, Frank Clement, Sammy Davis and the rest: but his handling of the TT Vauxhall along with Parry Thomas and George Duller brought added lustre to the name of Vauxhall.

The other memory I have is of Sir Charles John Bartlett, M.I.M.E., M.I.P.E., F.I.I.A., former managing director and chief architect of Vauxhall Motors, a man who might seem to the outside world far less dramatic than Brooklands drivers of Vauxhall TT's. Yet he was in reality the cornerstone of Vauxhall and Vauxhall cars today might be produced by a very different organisation if it had not been for Sir Charles Bartlett's dynamic influence.

During the Bartlett era I had many occasions to meet him either at Luton or at Whitewalls, his family home at Kingsbourne Green in Hertfordshire. Farming, horticulture of every sort, sport of every sort: that's the way the conversation would run, especially if he wanted to dodge direct Press enquiries on a Vauxhall or General Motors policy matter not finalised for world release. This rather remarkable man always seemed to have encyclopaedic knowledge of many topics other than car production and factory management. He was as interested as Lord Nuffield in medical matters and was an active member of the Industrial Health Research Board of the Medical Research Council; and because he believed in a happy working life stemming from contentment in the home, he was notoriously a fighter on the council of the Town and Country Planning Association.

In that shrewd, impartial survey of the motor industry

already mentioned in Chapter 3, Graham Turner's *The Car Makers* (Eyre & Spottiswoode), the following comment is made: 'In the 1920's Vauxhall was not noticeably different from the hire-and-fire employer then typical of the motor trade. "It was hell in those days," one old worker recalled. "I've seen men sacked for washing their hands just as the hooter blew . . . " But then, when most empires were reluctant to yield up their tyrannies and make way for an age when the unions shared their power, Vauxhall produced one of the most enlightened managers of his generation, Sir Charles Bartlett . . . Bartlett left Vauxhall in 1953, and to hear men talk you might think his reign was just a golden memory. The recollections are tireless in their adulation. "Bartlett was a gentleman—he was for the worker;" "I'm a Socialist and I shall die one, but whether you liked the bosses or not, you had to respect Charles Bartlett"; "Charlie Bartlett's door was always open"; "a man before his time, very subtle and imaginative". The comments come from hard-bitten shop stewards about a man who ruled over them for upwards of 20 years. . . .'

Moreover, as Graham Turner summarises the Vauxhall situation, Charles Bartlett left behind him the Management Advisory Committee, set up in 1941, which until recent times kept the entire Vauxhall organisation relatively free from industrial strife. In Charlie Bartlett's era the factory was split into over 20 areas, and a secret ballot enabled a representative from each to be elected. Everyone agreed this could only be done by a secret ballot, for otherwise some workers might be penalised.

Bartlett held monthly meetings with the MAC representatives (they retired automatically after a three-year term, but were eligible for re-election), together with six management representatives. Sir Reginald Pearson, an expert on industrial processes, a hard-hitting Midlander, spent nearly three-quarters of his working time on industrial relation matters, and continued the Bartlett tradition.

The one thing Sir Charles Bartlett did not encourage was personal discussion about himself. The Vauxhall mattered, not Charlie Bartlett. The result was that very few knew much about his personal life, except that he was knighted in 1944 in recognition of his own and Vauxhall's contribution to the war effort.

The surprising thing is that he made his way to the top in automobile engineering and a vast industrial complex, for he was at heart an accountant, a man of cold figures and not warm human industrial relationships. Gloucestershire-born, he went to Bath Technical College, trained in business methods with accounting specialisation, and in 1921 became accounting clerk with General Motors Ltd., the London-based British subsidiary of the General Motors Corporation. The year after GM acquired Vauxhall, Bartlett was transferred to Luton, and became Managing Director of Vauxhall Motors in 1930. At that time his little empire on what was jokingly called the Bedfordshire turnip patch was only 11 acres in extent. It employed 2,700 people and turned out 8,930 cars a year. By the time he gave up active control in 1953–4, he had 14,500 on the Luton payroll, and 130,000 Vauxhall cars and Bedford trucks were being produced annually. Today, as we have already seen, the payroll is more than doubled, and in addition to the 120,000 or so vehicles going for export there is in a normal good year an even greater total of 200,000 produced for the domestic market.

I talked to many who were close to Bartlett during those years, and as the industrial world has changed since then neither the Vauxhall management nor the unions may like much of what was said, nor of what actually happened. History will judge.

'When I first joined Luton in 1935,' one present executive told me, 'I was a member of the firm's football team. This was right at the end of the season when they were already playing cricket on the sports ground. I'll never forget when I walked into the pavilion and saw a kindly-faced man with steel-grey hair who asked me why I was off the field. I told him that the referee had stopped the game because the opposing team kept arguing. He was in whites, and asked me if I played cricket. On being told I did, he just laughed and said: "Well, then you'll have to join us!" At that time I didn't know who this very approachable man was. It never dawned on me he was the boss.'

Another told me: 'I don't suppose the present generation knows or cares, but Charlie Bartlett's time was the era of Vauxhall engineering leadership. We were the first with synchromesh gearchange, introduced from Detroit. And Vauxhalls had the American-inspired independent front suspension, while, of course, before 1937 we had the first British volume-produced car with an integral body. The five-day week was then just coming in, but we went on making those craftsmanlike cars without any strikes or troubles. Nobody had ever seen joint consultations like Charlie Bartlett's. . . .'

Another present executive said: 'Under Sir Charles there wasn't a strike for 20 years. We called them "Pauses for Consultation". You can laugh, but that's really what they were. Nobody lost any money. We were paid while the work stopped and the MAC (Management Advisory Committee) went into the trouble squarely.

'We called those 22 sections the "constituencies." There were only 21 at first, until Sir Charles went into it all to get complete representation. You see, he knew and really understood that you can't put all Vauxhall workers—or any car-factory workers —into a single group as "us", with the bosses as "them". For example, the press-shop, dealing in sheet steel, has quite different craft abilities, skills and problems from the constituencies dealing with stampings, forgings and machine tools, or the clerical staff in the different grades, or the production-line workers skilled and semi-skilled.

'Sir Charles insisted that the minutes of all MAC meetings

should be posted up throughout the works, so everyone *knew*. He started the works magazine, which now prints 50,000 copies. Of course the inevitable happened, and Vauxhall killed him. He died on 10th August the year after he retired from here. . . .'

How true is this legend of the era of Vauxhall engineering leadership? Of course, it has been re-created in modern times with the fantastic development of the Viva-type engine, new transmission systems and so forth. One of the Luton executives just quoted handed me a letter recently received from a Vauxhall owner in Auckland, New Zealand. 'For the last seven years I have owned a 1928 T–type Vauxhall Hurlingham sports', it read. 'I have ascertained that my car arrived in New Zealand on the ship *Tainui* on 16th January, 1930. . . . It was one of four Hurlinghams imported to this country. I have acquired three other engines and various back-ends, and hope to keep the car going for many years. . . . A short while ago I went with my wife to Taupo, on the shores of Lake Taupo, 179 miles from Auckland. It was mid-winter, and the southern part of North Island had the heaviest fall of snow for many years, with 18 degrees of frost. We arrived home having had no trouble of any kind with the car. Obviously a Vauxhall. . . .'

This was typical of Vauxhall reliability. Following the GM/ Vauxhall alliance in 1925 the accent shifted from low-volume high-cost cars to popular models for the fast-growing family-motoring market of the '30's, but devotees of other British-made cars were quickly disillusioned when they tried to use expressions such as 'tinny Yankee rubbish' about these products. Not only were the cars well built of good-quality materials, but there were powerful forces at Luton eager to hit back at critics.

These forces were led by the remarkable Arthur Francis Palmer Phillips, a University College ex-journalist who joined Sir Charles Bartlett quite early on as Sales Director, held that post for 24 years, and was accepted on both sides of the Atlantic as Vauxhall Motors' mouthpiece and champion.

When Sir Charles came over to Luton with GM there was a 'pause for consultation' while plans were introduced for the quite-different Vauxhalls with new American-based engineering impetus. The first major fruit of the GM/Vauxhall link was the Cadet, introduced for 1930, a low-priced model aimed at less-wealthy motorists. The Cadet was offered with 17 hp and 26 hp engine options, priced at £280–295. In 1931, a year after its introduction, the Cadet became the first British car to have a synchromesh gearbox. Then the big, tough 'Silent 80' of 1931–2 was in a way a transitional model between the high-priced cars of pre-GM days and the popular models headed by the Cadet. The '80' had a 23 hp six-cylinder engine, sold with various coachwork styles at up to £750. Its passing in 1932 firmly marked the end of the Luton period of building expensive Vauxhalls for a small, select market.

In 1933, following the Cadet in the popular class came the A-type Light Six. Again there were options, and the Light Six owner could have it in 12 hp form at only £195, or 14 hp at £215. This latter proved the more popular. I recall that on announcement day 250 Light Sixes were collected from Luton by Vauxhall dealers. This was not a Press stunt, but it was certainly unprecedented achievement in those days. The Light Six stayed in production until 1935, and Palmer Phillips told me with pride somewhere around 1933 that as many as 40 per cent of all 14 hp new car registrations in Britain were Vauxhalls.

In addition to refinements for the Light Six models, two Big Six Vauxhalls came out in 1934. These were the BY and BX models of 20 and 26 hp respectively. The larger was remarkable value at £325; both were well engineered and long-lasting, and many were seen around, as limousines and even as taxis, right up to the outbreak of the war in Britain. The 14 hp DX and the 12 hp DY launched in 1935 introduced independent front suspension for the first time on a popular medium-priced British car, and its success pushed up Vauxhall sales in 1935 to more than 26,000 cars. The price was only £205 for the 12 hp DY. Both models were produced up to 1938. The G-type of 1936 was really a big brother to the 10 hp model which for various reasons was not announced until 1937. Options, again. You could have short- or long-wheelbase G-types, and the philosophy of Sir Charles Bartlett was to give the public a large and comfortable 25 hp model, able to attain 80 mph, yet giving an average of 20 mpg. It was, nevertheless, a generous-budget car at £330 with a full specification including heater, fog and reversing lamps and other accessories.

Then in 1937 came the so-successful and at first so-controversial Ten, known at Luton as the H-type. It was the first British popular car produced on the integral construction principle, and one of the most advanced small cars of its day, yet costing only £158. In 1938 came a variant, the 12 hp I-type six-light saloon, but production of the 'Ten' continued up to 1940, by which time the Vauxhall plant was deeply involved in the war effort. The I-type was merged with the H-type after the war, when the latter became a 12 hp car. And in 1938—an unhappy time, as it turned out, to launch an important new model for the 1939 market—Luton produced the J-type, a 14 hp car which hardly went into production before the European side of the Second World War broke out. It was reintroduced after the war, and had a very advanced specification for its period. The smooth six-cylinder 1,781 cc engine gave an easy 30 mpg, and a top speed in the 70's. Features included an adjustable steering-column, double-acting shock-absorbers, no-draught ventilation, and such niceties as seat armrests and adjustable footrests—all for £220.

Nowadays, with our smooth-lift-off automatic transmissions, over-drive, servo brakes and all the rest, it is easy to forget that 40 years ago most cars did not have even a synchromesh box. As a long-service Vauxhall executive pointed out to me when we were examining Luton's collection of historic cars; 'The introduction of synchromesh from our American parent

Above. The mammoth General Motors' headquarters being completed in Detroit, in 1920, five years before GM acquired Vauxhall. *Below*. A 'Vauxhall' that might have been. Before obtaining control of Vauxhall, GM considered its own production of compact cars. This experimental baby car was designed for GM Research in 1925 by Fabio Sergadi (at wheel), but never put into production.

Above. In the late 1920's, Vauxhall contemplated quantity production of this advanced-design motor-cycle, an air-cooled four-cylinder
machine, with shaft drive.
Below. Series 101 Victor body, 1964, undergoing deflection tests for
rigidity. Amount of deflection as a load of 1,500 lb is applied is indicated in thousandths of an inch.

Above. 'The Vauxhall and West Hydraulic Engineering Co. Ltd.' works at Luton ('and offices Leadenhall Street, London') soon after the move to Luton in 1905.
Below. Craftsmen assembling a GM chassis in Detroit, in 1922, a scene which discounts any view that the long-established Vauxhall company was acquired by mass-producers of 'tinware'.

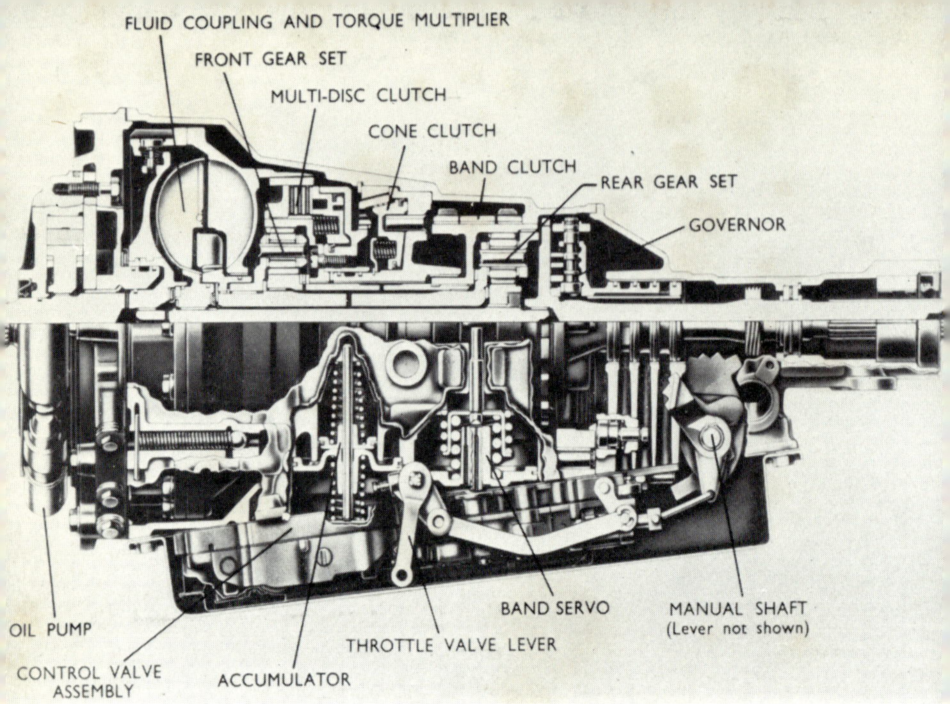

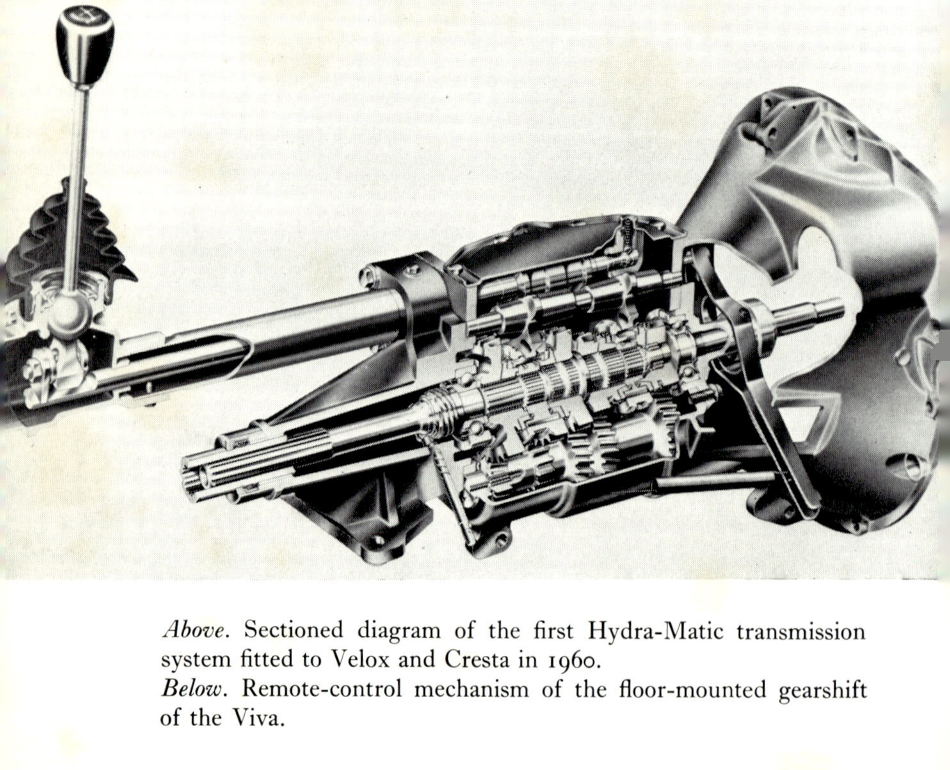

Above. Sectioned diagram of the first Hydra-Matic transmission system fitted to Velox and Cresta in 1960.
Below. Remote-control mechanism of the floor-mounted gearshift of the Viva.

company was in its way as important a step as the introduction of the electric self-starter—which also was a major Detroit pioneering project, first used on Cadillac. For the first time it meant that every woman could drive a car. In the distant past she could not swing an engine over by hand, but even after the self-starter there was the problem of changing gear. Our synchromesh cured most of the problem.

'Then there was economy. Although one could buy petrol at under a shilling a gallon, fuel consumption and the whole motoring budget were very important because millions of lower-income families were starting for the first time to own a car. With the help of Zenith, Vauxhall really got down to economy, and Palmer Phillips proved this, not just by issuing Press hand-outs but by setting up little one-gallon test units at various dealers. Ordinary motorists were getting fantastic economy—on occasions as much as 70 mpg with the Ten.'

Pardonable exaggeration? I have one of the Company's official releases of 1938, and what Palmer Phillips actually said was: 'Most Vauxhall dealers have special test tanks and fitments, and will place a car at the disposal of anyone who wishes to test the petrol consumption of a Vauxhall Ten. Thousands of motorists have made such tests, and we are getting figures so much in excess of 40 mpg that we would never dare to quote them. . . .'

Press correspondents took the Ten out, and only one achieved less than 40 mpg. He got 36·4 mpg. The average of all Press tests at that time worked out at 43·9 mpg.

Nowadays when giant car corporations rush to their legal departments at slight provocation, and when newspaper and television advertising codes ban certain claims and also criticisms which could be actionable, it is interesting to look back to the '30's and see how a powerful executive like Palmer Phillips coped with the situation when more than one large rival concern based in Britain was anxious to stifle Luton progress.

At one period the Ten was being badly knocked by critics, so he issued his retort: '*For the Information of the Motor Trade —the truth about the Vauxhall Ten.*'

No punches were pulled. 'In the course of a recent investigation to find out what the trade are saying about the Vauxhall Ten,' he said, 'we discovered that certain criticisms (or shall we say definite kinds of crabbing?) cropped up rather regularly. They mostly emanated from those in the trade whose financial interest is to sell other makes of 10 hp car. These criticisms were undoubtedly given in good faith, but were based on inaccurate information. . . .'

He found that the trade was being told by rumour-mongers: 'Independent springing is just a publicity stunt. . . It is not necessary on small cars . . . It gives a lot of trouble, and is not necessary on English roads.'

The Palmer Phillips retort to the 'publicity stunt' jibe was this: 'Before introducing the system on the 12 hp and 14 hp models for the 1935 season we had spent a very considerable period and a lot of money upon preliminary research work. The introduction of the new suspension meant entirely redesigning the cars and installing new machine tools and equipment. It also meant taking the risk that motorists might be prejudiced against the new idea by criticism which was bound to be put forward by interested parties. Any publicity man who suggested such drastic steps purely as a stunt would not keep his job long. Since we pioneered independent front-wheel springing on a popular British car each successive Vauxhall has been equipped with independent springing, and over 100,000 happy owners can tell you whether it is just a publicity stunt or not.'

More serious were criticisms that ifs would put up insurance rates and that 'a bad accident will wreck the car'.

Palmer Phillips promptly quizzed every reputable company transacting motor insurance, from Alliance Assurance to Zurich General Accident, including all major tariff, non-tariff and Lloyds companies, and asked them to send engineers along before issuing rates. As a result it was found that no company charged more than the standard 10 hp rate. While individual rates naturally varied, all were normal or even below normal for the class of car.

Rumours that a bad accident would wreck a car with ifs were promptly stopped when, for reasons totally unconnected with the car, a Vauxhall Ten owner did have a bad crash. The insurance engineers sent the following report to Luton: 'Last week we had our first claim reported, in which one of your 10 hp cars was involved in a serious head-on collision. . . . Until I saw the result of the impact on the above car I was dubious as to how far back the damage would be transmitted by the diagonal bracing which transfers the load from the sub-frame to the front body assembly and the roof.

'I am pleased, however, to be able to report that although the head-on impact was severe enough entirely to destroy the radiator, distort the front end of the assembly sub-frame and force the engine from its mounting, no damage has occurred behind the diagonal tube bracing.' (These are the body front-end brace rods which unite the sub-frame and integral body into one rigid structure.) 'From the extent of the damage to the front end, I have formed the opinion that if this car had been fitted with a conventional chassis frame there would have been distortion of the off-side member beyond the scuttle dash.'

This disproved the suggestion that the Vauxhall construction held potential danger. While one does not associate the pre-war Vauxhall with international rally success, part of the initial testing of the Ten was an unofficial entry by a Stour-bridge team for the 1938 Monte Carlo Rally. The car covered 2,275 miles without losing a single mark, in spite of the fact that much of the route was over snow and ice-bound roads of the usual Monte degree of toughness. The car was driven hard, put up a good showing in the final acceleration trials, and the tool-kit was not touched. This was in January, 1938, barely two months after Luton production of the series began.

When Vauxhall introduced ifs, and simultaneously brought the phrase 'knee-action' into the automobile engineers' dictionary, the publicity line from 1935 onwards was '*Riding changed to Gliding*'. Captain W. Gordon Aston, then motoring correspondent of *The Times*, took a 'knee-action' Light Six out on an extended test, and the whole of Sir Charles Bartlett's team must have been gratified to read Gordon Aston's opinions that: 'Not only a step forward but a real stride has been made in technical progress', and: 'The Vauxhall engine reaches an enviably high standard of refinement.' This was, in truth, the start of the era of Vauxhall engineering achievement, and the era itself is a memorial to Sir Charles Bartlett.

After his retirement in 1953 the US-based parent company appointed two American chief executives in turn, and they were followed by a very strong Yorkshire-born chief, William Swallow. His name is still something of a byword at Vauxhalls. He started his working life in a Huddersfield motor engineering business which his father considered had greater prospects than the preceding family interest in Yorkshire textile machinery. Bill Swallow joined General Motors in 1947 and spent nearly two years in the United States. This gave him a permanent 'transatlantic' accent, half Huddersfield, half Michigan. For a period he had worked with a steel group now part of the British-Leyland organisation, when his boss had been Len Lord, later to become Lord Lambury, K.B.E.

Of course, there are very many thousands of pre-1966 Vauxhalls on the road throughout the world, and most of these are cars built during Bill Swallow's time at Vauxhall, which was also contemporary with George Harriman at BMC, the Hon. Geoffrey Rootes at Rootes, and Donald Stokes at Standard-Triumph. Since then there have been more mergers, knighthoods and peerages throughout the car industry, but Vauxhall reverted to being run by a much-honoured American executive who could therefore not be honoured on the British pattern. In January 1966 David L. Hegland came to Vauxhall as Chairman and Managing Director. At 50 he presents an English appearance to those meeting him for the first time, which was not surprising perhaps. Although born in Great Falls, Montana, and a GM man since 1945, he held GM appointments all through Europe—Sweden, Belgium, Germany, Denmark—before going on to South Africa and Australia.

To Vauxhall, Hegland brought a new international understanding and outlook, vital to Britain as a major exporting nation.

7

Gasoline Buggy Town

Of course today's Vauxhall owner is intrigued by the hurdy-gurdies and twinkling tree-top coloured candle-lights of Vauxhall Gardens. He is proud to think of Vauxhalls stemming from the fine heritage of those Prince Henry models which roared along Russian and German highways, and of 30/98's high on the concrete of the Brooklands Byfleet banking.

But when he turns to his own modern Vauxhall of steel-plate and chrome trim, its engine partly assembled by robot transfer machines, its torque-converter automatic transmission a near-miracle of engineering ingenuity, he says: 'This is *now*. This is British made, inspired by Detroit, as ultra-modern as a computer or a satellite space capsule.'

Yes, this is a correct modern viewpoint, but it overlooks the fascinating story of Detroit, which is not only the hub of the world's motor industry, but has links which are part of British, French and Canadian history. When the first gasoline buggy chuffed its way through the city's streets, Detroit was already antient, in a way of which most European visitors are totally ignorant. I went there for the first time in the '50's to explore the ramifications of 'the greatest factory in the world', and found myself entranced, exploring Detroit's rich past just as American tourists do in Europe when they see Windsor Castle, Hampton Court Palace, or walk down the Royal Mile to Holyrood.

Most first-timers in Detroit who have not bothered to look at a map are astounded to discover they can board a bus and for a buck or two be driven *south* into Canada. The solution of this puzzle is found in the geographical shape of the Great Lake borders which right here place Windsor, Ontario, at a more southerly latitude than Detroit. Moreover, first-timers who expect to find nothing but skyscrapers and steelworks are surprised at the beauty of the Rouge River, the boulevards, the Detroit Institute of Arts, and the startling architectural palace of the Cultural Center. Some of this does not square up, it is true, with riot-torn and squalid zones of other parts of Detroit, but that is a story for someone else to tell.

Again, the first-timer bored at school by history-books is certain to be puzzled at the preponderance of French place-names, and the sudden realisation that Cadillac is not merely a luxury car for plutocrats but also the name of a city square, and a mammoth hotel, and all of these commemorate the commander and founder of Detroit, Antoine La Mothe Cadillac, who came from Gascony in south-western France. His native village, unlike Detroit, remains little changed, and the house in which he was born on 5th March, 1658, is still occupied as a dwelling. The rough acre-square log stockade which Cadillac built in the heart of the American wilderness some 250 years ago, hoping that it would one day become a powerful centre of trade and commerce, is now the site of Detroit's futurist-looking Civic Center.

Dig deep, as I did, if this little-known (to Europeans) aspect of American history has a strong appeal. Budding writers of Westerns will find it a fruitful source of characters and plots, for after Champlain (known to millions in Canada as The Father of the New France) led the way to the Great Lakes, he appointed 21-year-old Jean Nicolet to 'master the language and ways of life of the savages', and he spent the next 10 years as a lone white resident among the Indians of Michigan at the Straits of Mackinac. In 1671 scores of Indian tribes totalling some 2,000 men witnessed the formal annexation to France at a ceremony in Sault Saint Marie, where (according to Milo M. Quaife, author of many books on early Detroit): 'Volleys of musketry were discharged, the Royal arms were affixed to a cross planted in the ground, and Father Allouez delivered an oration extolling the glory of the French King and the omnipotence of his armies.'

Vauxhall enthusiasts do not have to concern themselves with the many battles which followed for nearly two centuries, although their dates have to be painfully remembered by many an American schoolboy: there is only one date which a British visitor to Detroit finds sad to recall, and this is 1796, the year when after various changes of fortune Detroit was in the hands of the British, and a garrison of redcoats occupied Fort Lernoult despite the fact that the Treaty of Paris had officially put an end to the Revolutionary War, and the new boundary put Detroit on American soil. Again, the battles between the 3,000-strong army of General Wayne, the militia-men from Detroit and the Ottawa, Chippewa and Delaware braves ought to come out of the history books and be re-created in novels and screened dramas. As Milo Quaife says: 'No other American city has experienced such vicissitudes as this one. Twice it has endured the horrors of an Indian siege; twice it has surrendered to conquering armies; five times its flag has changed. Three different nations have claimed its allegiance; repeatedly it has been ravaged by epidemics and financial panics; once it was burned completely to the ground.'

In the gas-lit days before the sparking DC of Detroit-Edison, before there were great stores and luxury offices on Wood-ward Avenue, the hub of Detroit was the Russell House, where any member of the male sex of legal age could walk right in and be served with draught beer for five cents, or a double whiskey for twenty-five. This was when the gasoline buggy first appeared on Detroit streets, but in the pioneering days the most glamorous episode grew from the American visit of the Prince of Wales, later King Edward VII. He made his entry to Detroit via Windsor, with full escort brought by ferry across the Rouge.

'A tremendous press of people met him at the foot of Woodward', said Detroit historian George W. Stark. 'The Prince knew not whether to be terrified or delighted. He had never experienced the temperament of an American crowd, but he had read things. He was driven to Russell House, a milling mob tagging the royal carriage. He succeeded in getting to his rooms, but the crowd swarmed about the hotel and blocked the streets. The Prince was persuaded to walk out on the balcony and speak briefly. The Prince was charming. The crowd was satisfied and soon dispersed. An early hands-across-the-sea gesture had been happily completed. . . .'

It was this Prince who became the first Monarch to drive an automobile (albeit a Daimler, not a Vauxhall), and it was this same glittering old hotel in the hub of Detroit which became the centre of the world motor business. I quote from Stark's *In Old Detroit*: 'Calling the roll of the Pontchartrain bar would be something similar to calling the roll of the kings of the motor industry of the present day . . . Life was not all beer and skittles, even in the Pontchartrain. Men gathered there from the four corners of the earth. It was a new quest. Fortunes were being gambled. Men playing hard, but they also worked desperately. Peter Drexelius, master of the destinies of the old Pontchartrain bar back then, remembers that it was no uncommon sight to see four or five men carry a heavy piece of machinery into the room, place it on the floor and set it in motion. He even remembers the day that Albert Champion, newly arrived from France, walked in with an elaborate electric set and with vast Latin enthusiasm showed a group of strangers his *superieur* porcelain for spark-plugs. Everything was shown off in the Pontchartrain bar: tyre vulcanisers, rims, valves, brakes, carburetters, magnetos and whatnot. . . .'

Many years later, in 1956, when Detroit's J. L. Hudson Company was celebrating its 75th year, I inspected the working

G

replica which Hudson's had constructed of one of the first automobiles to appear on Detroit's streets. Its exciting development ran a close parallel to that of Hudson's, which began as a small men's-wear shop in the Detroit Opera House and became one of the world's largest stores.

'Come quick! He's driving down State Street in some crazy contraption,' was the theme of the reconstruction of the actual day when Charles Brady King, a marine gas-engine builder and friend of Henry Ford, drove his first car at six miles an hour.

For several years he had experimented with his gasoline buggy in a workshop in Jefferson Avenue, and by March, 1896, it was ready for its first outdoor test-run. As he was the only one prepared for the event, it caused an immediate sensation, and crowds gathered to laugh and point at the spindly little wagon bouncing down State Street. After that day the police ordered him to test the car only at Belle Isle, where there were only rough tracks limiting the speed to five miles an hour—and King had boasted that the buggy could do 20.

After organising the Northern Motor Car Company and the King Motor Car Company, Charles Brady King retired to his other hobbies, art and music, and let the coming princes of the car industry wage their race for power.

America had already been invaded by European cars. In his *My Life and Work*, written in collaboration with Samuel Crowther, Henry Ford said: 'Others in this country and abroad were building cars by that time, and in 1895 I heard that a Benz car from Germany was on exhibition in Macy's store in New York. I travelled down to look at it, but it had no features that seemed worth while.'

Neither Brady nor Ford were actually the first men to drive their own car around the present General Motors area, however. The question of priority is naturally a vital one in Detroit, and in 1949 it was researched by the Automobile Manufacturers' Association which gave definite priority to the brothers Charles and Frank Duryea, whose buggy ran in 1893. A Haynes car was placed second, Brady third (1896) and Ford three months after Brady. These findings are substantially in agreement with those of the Smithsonian Institution, where the original Duryea and Haynes car may now be seen. Ford's earliest is in the Ford Museum.

Some of this past living legend of the Detroit car industry may hold the interest of those who daub anti-American slogans on walls—or who, at the other extreme, imagine nothing ever happened in the United States prior to stainless steel, solid-state and space travel. For such misunderstandings some Americans themselves are to blame. For example, the moguls of the mighty General Motors Corporation simply cannot understand that outside their vastness there are millions of meek men who feel battered about the head by GM's vital statistics such as: 'World-wide capital expenditures for plant and equipment, $860 million . . . total dollar sales of all products, $20,208,505,000. . . .'

Size is not the key to understanding GM, although these statistics stagger imagination. In most recent years the total GM budget for any twelvemonth exceeds the national budget of a nation such as France. Its average number of employees with their families outnumber the population of, say, New Zealand.

We are looking at Detroit and at General Motors because, like it or not, this colossus owns Vauxhall. It must be clearly understood that while the capital now is American, much of it (as we saw in an earlier chapter) is ploughed back into Britain for research, development, and to make better, larger and more profitable conditions for British workers at Vauxhall plants. In no other sense is the Vauxhall car 'American'. It is British designed, British researched and tested, and largely made (to about the same proportion as any other car manufactured in Britain) from British materials.

There is complete interchange between Detroit and Luton executives, and while it is obvious that American styling has influenced Vauxhall and indeed most major car manufacturers, it is an intelligent Vauxhall owner who tries, just in this chapter and the next, to see the world picture from the Detroit viewpoint.

'General Motors is basically a very simple company,' is the way GM's chairman Frederic G. Donner once put it. 'We are fundamentally a company that designs, builds and sells products based on motors.'

Commenting on this, *Newsweek* said: 'The thousands of hours spent trying to analyse General Motors, the millions of words written about it by industry experts, financial wizards and academicians would seem to belie chairman Donner's apparently offhand remark . . . From the flivver-making days it has become an international organisation of colossal size. . . . In recent years its character has become diffuse as its bosses tended away from the flamboyance of a Charles Wilson or a Harlow Curtice. GM has presented no public face except the goblin grimaces of its automobile grilles. . . .'

So vast is America that, since the pioneering days at which we have been looking in Detroit, more than 2,500 different makes of motor-cars have been produced in the United States at one time or another, and today only a handful remain. General Motors was organised in 1908, but its roots go back to the very earliest days of the industry and even beyond—to carriage and wagon-building, stationary engines and bicycle bells; to the days when men like R. E. Olds, David Buick and Henry Leland were experimenting with horseless carriages.

Today, when you look at the rest of the world through a GM window in Detroit, wondering how Vauxhall fits into this scene, you hear GM executives saying: 'We are an international organisation creating a better life in the world community. Through the Overseas Operations division, of global scope, GM exports its products to all parts of the free world. GM subsidiaries abroad manufacture cars, trucks, automotive parts. In that way GM contributes to the economic strength and technical resources of the 24 countries in which there are GM manufacturing, assembly or distribution facilities. It supplies managerial and engineering skills. It creates jobs. GM contributes tax revenues for the support of local and national governments.'

Of course, Luton and Ellesmere Port are dots on the world map at Detroit, comparable in many ways with other GM dots such as GM Argentina SA, GM de Mexico SA de CV, GM International A/S (Copenhagen) and GM New Zealand Limited; but in everything emanating from Detroit you see GM's pride reflected in the national individuality of its companies. There is absolutely no attempt to impose an American-way-of-life pattern on other countries.

Printed literature I was given in the New York office referred to the three main overseas car plants in the following terms: this was not specially slanted, nor intended primarily to be read at all in Britain: '*Vauxhall*: British good taste and workmanship are reflected in the three new Vauxhall lines . . . *Holden*: Smart, freshly designed, built in Australia and proved over Australia's rough terrain, the Holden is finding markets in many areas of the world . . . *Opel*: Opel's proud German heritage of over one hundred years is excitingly expressed in the three new lines, Kadett, Rekord and Admiral. . . .'

To sum it up, the outside world as seen from the GM Detroit HQ is explained to Americans by GM in this way: 'General Motors' three "made-abroad" cars, designed to meet the needs of their home countries, have also found wide acceptance in other nations throughout the Free World. In addition to their wide range of passenger cars, both Adam Opel AG and General Motors-Holden's Pty Limited produce light commercial vehicles, and Vauxhall Motors Limited produces the Bedford, one of Europe's most popular line of vans, trucks and coaches. Nearly half the annual output of the Opel and Vauxhall plants is exported to more than 100 countries, with many of these vehicles shipped in knocked-down form for assembly in other General Motors plants. Beside the rapidly increasing production of Opels, Holdens and Vauxhalls, American-designed vehicles adapted to local conditions are being manufactured in Brazil and Argentina.'

I repeat: the Vauxhall is British designed, British researched and tested, and largely made by British citizens from almost entirely British materials. But that there is great industrial and international strength in such a mammoth group as General Motors is surely obvious. Even GM is a little apprehensive of its own vastness, and *Newsweek* commented: 'It isn't simply a question of power, although eight anti-Trust Division lawyers brood full time over the General Motors industrial complex.' Anti-trust in this sense means anti-monopoly: and in a recent *Spotlight on Business*, GM's sheer vastness was summarised thus: 'Profits last year were the most massive *ever recorded by any company—anywhere. . . .* General Motors' Federal income tax of $1·3 billion would just about pay for a year's operation, including salaries, of the entire Congress, the Federal judicial system, the White House, the Treasury Department and the Justice Department—including the anti-Trust Division! Every working day last year General Motors sold 20,956 cars, trucks and buses, a daily line of vehicles that would stretch, bumper to bumper, more than 70 miles.'

Wise, internationally-minded Vauxhall owners may feel pride in this great family through which by their choice of car they belong. It cannot be denied there is still a comparative handful of vintage motorists who wish it were some other company than Vauxhall (of Prince Henry and 30/98 past glories) which GM had brought up. And it very nearly was another company—Austin Motors.

The Austin Seven had not been introduced, the car which ultimately brought Austin finances out of the red, and for quite some time Sir Herbert Austin (as he then was) brooded on the golden opportunity he turned down when the GM offer went from Longbridge to Luton. I remember him complaining to my former colleague Arthur C. Armstrong, editor of *The Motor*: 'Just think—I was offered £700,000 for my interest in the company. And I could have retired on that!'

8

Two and a half Million Bucks

Other people's money is always a fascinating subject, especially if it runs into many thousands. If we concede, as we must, that it was a very good thing for British workers and British industry that General Motors bought out Vauxhall Motors when they did, then Vauxhall motorists cannot fail to ask: 'How big was the deal?'

The short answer to that question is: 'Two and a half million bucks', but to know what sort of bargain it was, if any, you need to have the story told by the man who fixed the international deal. This was Alfred P. Sloan, Jr., one of the most distinguished GM men, President from 1923 to 1937, Chairman until April, 1956, and Honorary Chairman until his death in 1966. This prominent American had an enormous influence upon the future of Vauxhall, and all that Sir Charles Bartlett was able to build for the British company was done with Sloan's backing.

Alfred P. Sloan, Jr, was born in 1875, and graduated from MIT (Massachusetts Institute of Technology, today a household name around the world, as the result of the space race) when he was only 20. He joined the Hyatt Roller Bearing Company at the beginning of motoring in the United States, and when in time Hyatt was merged with several other car-component companies to form the United Motors Corporation, he was its president. In 1918 United became part of the General Motors group, of which Sloan was appointed President and Chief Executive in 1923. In the United States not only much of GM's greatness but also the Alfred P. Sloan Foundation and the Sloan-Kettering Institute for Cancer Research are memorials to him.

In 1961–2 he decided to write a series of essays on American business, with special relation to GM, and gathered around him a writing team headed by John McDonald (then editor of *Fortune* magazine) and Catherine Stevens. At various times they were joined by the sociologist Nathan Glazer, Jason Epstein, Sidney S. Alexander of MIT, Ralph Stein, author of *Sports Cars of the World*, and many more, each contributing a facet to the proposed essays. Sloan later admitted: 'As we got into a study of the facts, the project grew far beyond our original concept.' The complex GM story could be told only with the life of Alfred Sloan as its central theme, since he had spent more than 65 years in and around the automobile industry, 45 of them in GM. His father was a wholesale tea, coffee and cigar merchant in New Haven, Connecticut, who moved to new premises on West Broadway, New York City, when Alfred was 10, so the family background was Brooklyn. Ultimately the writing project which Sloan's team began emerged as *My Years with General Motors* (Doubleday & Co. Inc.), on which the following insight into the Vauxhall deal is based.

Now that Britain has a relatively fixed annual HP tax (the owner's total annual fiscal outlay being controlled chiefly by petrol tax), it is apt to be forgotten that for many years prior to the Second World War there was the ill-based £1-a-horse-power duty which was to the benefit of 'light cars', as they were then called, but restrictive to larger and more comfortable cars. It was one reason why elderly but desirable Silver Ghosts and Phantom's reached only £50 or so on the used-car market, and many a powerful used American car could be bought for less. Thus, in the 1920's the American market in Britain was difficult. There were the McKenna duties which raised tariff barriers against Buick, Essex, Chrysler and others just as against Mercedes-Benz, Hispano-Suiza and Renault and the rest. Indeed, the Americans were worse hit, since the RAC formula penalised the 'square' (almost equal bore and stroke) low-revving Detroit type of power unit, compared with the long-stroke and relatively smaller-bore engines of the European designers.

When Sloan had a British survey made in 1924 it was found that these factors—and more especially the £1-a-horsepower tax—resulted in a typical British-made family saloon such as the Austin costing an average of eleven shillings a week (roughly $138 a year then) for standing charges, compared with £1 a week (then about $250 annually) for a typical American family sedan such as the Chevrolet.

In parenthesis it ought to be said that Chevvie nowadays is one of the most popular cars in the United States. It began in 1911, hand-built in a rented workshop on Detroit's West Grand Boulevard. Only some 3,000 were produced in the first year. The name of Louis Chevrolet, a famous racing driver, of the period, did not seem to attract much public custom. In 1918 Chevrolet became the Chevrolet Motor Division of General Motors Corporation (bringing with it to GM the Scripps-Booth, today a much-prized vintage name), and for the first time GM had a car which was potentially competitive with Ford. Nevertheless for reasons which now need not concern Vauxhall owners, Chevvie at the outset was a headache for GM, and at one point in 1921 it was losing around $1 million a month. This was at the worst of the 'buddy-can-you-spare-a-dime' slump which indirectly triggered off the General Strike in Britain. Chevvie suffered during 1924 by not being given an improved specification, GM's overall sales dropped by 28 per cent, and it was not until the K-model Chevrolet of 1925 that the market rose. Total Chevvie sales for the year were 481,000. This was three times the annual sales of *all* cars in Britain. As an example Britain's industrial problems had caused Austin production to drop to only 1,000 cars a month in 1924.

Under pressure, the British government of the day suspended the McKenna duties in mid-1924, only to reimpose them during 1925. GM were well-established as assemblers of imported US components. During 1925–1932, GM (Hendon) assembled 17,884 cars (Cadillac, Buick, Chevrolet, Oakland and Maquette). Thousands of Bedfords were also built at Hendon. Charles Bartlett was engaged in this operation, as head of GM Ltd.

Alfred Sloan's right-hand man in the investigation was James D. Mooney, and he started negotiations with Longbridge to buy out Austin's, bringing to England with him one of the fathers of the American motor industry, Fred J. Fisher, of the distinguished Fisher family responsible for the Fisher Body Corporation (subsequently Fisher Body Division, GMC). Their proposition to Austin was £1 million to buy share control, plus preference-share rights and dividend coverage which would involve GM in having to pay out (in round figures) $5.5 million. In July, 1925, this was an enormous sum, but GM believed they could earn at least 20 per cent on the investment as well as protecting some interests of American manufacturers.

Arguments about the high finance continued for seven weeks, and as Austin's would not give way on the valuation of Longbridge assets a cable had to be sent to Detroit early in September that negotiations were off.

'As I recall the incident', wrote Alfred Sloan 38 years later in his Doubleday account, 'I was actually relieved to hear this news. For it seemed to me that Austin had largely the same disadvantages that had bothered me about Citroen six years earlier; its physical plant then was in poor condition and its management was weak. And I still had some doubts whether our own management was strong enough to make up for Austin's deficiencies; indeed, the continued dilution of our management strength as we expanded overseas and at home was a problem all during the 1920's. . . .'

Surely this is the answer to those who still misguidedly

think of GM as an American colossus which crossed the Atlantic to grab Vauxhall? When the Longbridge negotiations were broken off, a General Motors team comprising James D. Mooney, Fred Fisher and Donaldson Brown (a financial genius of GM's executive committee) opened discussions at Luton.

The official record of this today at Vauxhall is this: 'By the mid-20's the Vauxhall fortunes were ebbing. At this time, too, General Motors Corporation of America were looking for car-manufacturing facilities in Britain. It became obvious that a marriage should be arranged, to the very real benefit of both parties. Negotiations began, and after a time agreement was reached in 1925 under which General Motors acquired the entire ordinary share capital of Vauxhall Motors Limited.'

The official GM record, as expounded to Doubleday's by Alfred Sloan, was that this was a much less controversial matter than the Austin project. Vauxhall were manufacturing relatively high-priced cars (the nearest GM comparison, price-wise, was the Buick), with a yearly production of only around 1,500.

'It was in no sense a substitute for Austin,' Sloan said. 'Indeed, I looked on it as only a kind of experiment in overseas manufacturing. The experiment seemed appealing, however, and the investment required of us was only $2,575,291. . . .'

Amusing, perhaps, to ask now how that final one dollar arrived on the cheque. One would have thought that a deal of such magnitude might have been summarised to the nearest hundred dollars, to say the least.

Nothing happened immediately after the change. Hendon was booming, assembling US-made units, and there was no hurry to change the pattern of things at Luton. However, it is true the deal was signed in 1925, and it was October, 1931, before the first production of the General Motors/Vauxhall amalgamation appeared on the motoring scene in the shape of the Cadet at a basic £280. In Britain Sir Charles Bartlett was

working to consolidate all that was best at Luton and to reinforce it with the Detroit capital now available. Meanwhile, he
was in business producing in turn the 25/70, the 20/50 R-type,
and the 23 hp Silent 80 six-cylinder car, all fairly large and
expensive, showing no hint of a superimposition of Detroit
policy.

Not until he completed his autobiography in 1963 did
Alfred Sloan disclose the surprising fact that GM's executive
committee had no policy for Vauxhall—or to put it less bluntly,
in Sloan's own words: 'The committee had not yet crystallised
an overseas policy.' Vauxhall went on losing money for Detroit
in the first few years of the amalgamation.

Possibly the last man to be worried about this was Sloan
himself, never anxious for Detroit to go into Europe. In this
he was at loggerheads with James D. Mooney, who was not
especially pro-Britain, but firmly believed GM should be
decentralised throughout the world. Other GM VIP's believed
it was wrong for the corporation to manufacture away from
home, and that the companies they were acquiring should
be concerned solely with selling American products. Sloan
himself admitted in his autobiography: 'I was interested in a
suggestion that we create in the United States an organisation
to design a modified "small-bore" Chevrolet—a car that would
escape the heavy horsepower tax in England. . . . I felt that if
this were done, it might prove unnecessary to develop a new
small car at Vauxhall. . . .'

It was during June, 1928, that Vauxhall's fate was finally
determined, and to some extent this accounts for the delay
before Bartlett introduced his new model.

Of course it is easy to see that back home in the United
States the Chevvie was beating Ford, so a similar world
success might come from developing a small-bore Chevvie.
That such a car could ever have been successfully manufactured
or even assembled at Luton is now doubtful, although it ought
to be noted that until quite recent times American Fords

were being assembled at the Henry Ford works in Cork, Eire. It was James D. Mooney who convinced the GM management, using dollar arguments only, that there was a powerful case for expansion at Vauxhall. He confounded Detroit die-hards by giving Chevrolet figures proving that it was not the rival to Ford in overseas markets as it seemed on its home ground, and anyway in any country other than the United States the humble Chevvie cost up to 75 per cent more. Mooney also felt it necessary to protect their $2·5 million investment in Luton, and clinched the matter by explaining that the British Empire (such as Britain had in 1928) 'covered 38 per cent of the world markets outside of the United States and Canada, so it was important to consider England as a source for export markets'.

Alfred Sloan did not come over to Europe until October, 1928. He arrived accompanied by Charles T. Fisher (another of the famous Fisher brothers) and John Thomas Smith. Despite his English-sounding name, Smith was a Detroit man, an associate of William C. Durant, the Buick Motor Company head who helped to found GM on 16th September, 1908.

It makes comparison easier of we look at all the figures in dollars. Years previously, when Alfred Sloan's Hyatt Roller Bearing company was merged with Durant's interests, about $13·5 million changed hands. The Austin deal was not completed at $5·5 million, Vauxhall was acquired for $2·5 million. And by 1931 the Adam Opel family sold out to GM for $33 million. This latter deal was the result of a top-secret GM 'study group' meeting in Paris in March, 1929.

1931 was a significant time for Vauxhall Motors, because in that year the first Bedford commercial vehicle was launched. This was a small $1\frac{1}{2}$-ton model, but the Bedford range grew steadily. Bedford has become the world's biggest exporter of trucks, produced at Dunstable in the truck plant with the largest output in Europe. Meanwhile the change to mass-produced family cars was just what Vauxhall needed, and during the '30's under Bartlett's leadership the Company grew rapidly. By

1935, for instance, annual production had topped the 50,000 mark, and there were nearly 8,000 people (mostly men) on the Vauxhall payroll.

As this *Companion* volume is an independent book, written to put the facts before Vauxhall owners, and not necessarily in doing so to flatter either Vauxhall Motors or General Motors, it has to be said there are naturally many people in Detroit fearful of European politics. They were vocal when war came and the Adam Opel properties fell entirely into enemy hands; indeed the arguments in Europe continued for nearly two years after the war, until General Lucius Clay, the American military governor in the Allied Military Government, urged GM not to delay in taking their war-torn Opel properties back immediately, 'lest they pass to a custodian appointed by the German State', as Sloan explained.

At various times arguments continued as to whether GM should expand Vauxhall or (in 1928, specifically) 'write it off as a bad investment'. Events have proved the pro-Britain group right. They have been supported in the early years by two men in particular. One was Albert Bradley, a GM leader from 1923 and one-time chairman, born in Yorkshire, England. The other was Frederic Garrett Donner, later to become chairman.

In so far as GM finance helps Vauxhall's fortunes, Donner came to be linked with the sort of Vauxhall cars which you and I drive, but that does not primarily help you and me to understand a millionaire in Donner's unique position.

James Jones, who profiled him for Detroit's *Ward's Quarterly*, said: 'Frederic Garrett Donner is by no means as tough a man to get down on paper as some other prominent men, but he doesn't translate easily. He shuns personal publicity.' Nevertheless, James Jones gleaned facts about Donner's wife Eileen, his amateur-painting son and daughter, his home life at Port Washington, Long Island, and his mid-Manhattan apartment. An enigma to many, Donner is certain to provoke many a Vauxhall owner into thinking: 'How do you get a job like that?'

In fact Donner did serve behind a counter, in a small Michigan drugstore (ice-cream parlour and general store) where among other things he helped develop film and print snapshots. Today he is still a keen photographer. After emerging from Michigan University with a BA degree in business administration (somewhat similar to a British economics degree) he joined a Chicago firm of accountants, entering GM as a financial staff accountant in the New York office, in 1926. In due course he became executive vice-president of finance, to be succeeded in that position by George Russell as eventually Donner was appointed to the top job in GM. The present Chairman and Chief Executive Officer is James M. Roche.

When industrial arguments boil up in Vauxhall or in other GM-financed plants around the world, I have heard criticism that Detroit is too far away, that the moguls who sign the dollar-cheques have no idea what really goes on in countries outside the United States. This was never true of Frederic Donner, who has been many times around the world, from England to Australia, from California and Canada to Switzerland and South Africa, but always in touch with his personal office. As a subordinate told James Jones: 'He's never more than a phone's throw away.'

His personal wealth has never been disclosed. US balance sheets are not legally required to disclose executives' salaries or stock-holding, and these are among the best-kept secrets in the monster General Motors Building at Fifth Avenue and 58th, New York City. This is a 50-storey skyscraper of which GM hold the surprising (for New York) proportion of the first 26 floors.

Of course Donner never 'owned' Vauxhall nor General Motors. During heated political and industrial discussions foolish things are often said about multi-millionaire moguls. In the sense that GM 'owns' Vauxhall you and I 'own' GM.

Holders of the ordinary shares ('common stock', in American parlance) number some 1,270,000. In the United States about one-tenth of these holders are the big insurance, college and hospital institutions. Quite apart from private investors, many people in many countries would no doubt be surprised to know that their savings, their unit trusts, their insurance funds, and even the funds backing the mortgages and other money they've borrowed, have a tiny share of GM dividends. While GM is the biggest company of its kind in the world, it is not quite the biggest payer of dividends. That honour belongs to AT & T (American Telephone and Telegraph), a group world-famous because of its role in space travel.

Veteran and vintage-car enthusiasts sometimes wish they had been able to buy a Prince Henry new for around £585 in 1911, or a 30/98 new in 1919 for £1,950, and they try to calculate how much such treasures would be worth today at Sotheby's. It is even more intriguing to calculate what sort of millionaire you would now be had you invested some small savings in General Motors right at the start in 1908, kept that holding all through the slump, through the acquisition of Vauxhall, right to the present day.

There have been so many splits, rights issues and variations between the pound sterling and the dollar that exact comparison is impossible. Nevertheless, a financial expert, Felix Brunner, has calculated what might have happened if any of the original 355 shareholders in General Motors, in 1908, had the foresight to hold on. *None did.* But if you had put £250 into that gamble in September, 1908, kept all the dividends intact and taken up all your rights (these would have cost a further £9,000 or thereabouts), you would now hold 22,900 shares in GM, worth just under the £1 million, and you would have enjoyed dividends totalling £150,000 at least.

British Vauxhall owners, of course, are quite free to invest in GM at any time, and there is at least one advantage in doing so even though I must stress for the third time that the Vaux-

H

hall cars we drive are entirely designed and built in Britain. Treasury ruling prevents you from actually holding GM share certificates, which have to be lodged with an authority such as a bank, although Bearer Deposit receipts, and unit trusts (mutual funds) with an interest in GM may of course be held. Those with GM shares are sent three times a year an illustrated magazine-type of Shareholders' Quarterly, in addition to the lavish annual report. As I began this chapter by saying: 'Other people's money is always a fascinating subject' . . . especially when some of your own is invested in this $11·5-billion kitty.

9

Styling

As we see, the dollar investment of General Motors Corporation reinforces all that Vauxhall do in Britain, but there are many reasons other than the dollar why Vauxhall design and engineering are different from the American pattern.

Cynics may say that the Prince Henry and the 30/98 were not styled at all, but simply bolted together. Vauxhall's director of styling, David B. Jones, A.R.C.A., came to Luton in 1934, and the first Vauxhall he designed for the Company was the Ten coupé of 1937, with bodywork by Pressed Steel.

He told *Autocar*'s editor, Peter Garnier, recently that he joined Vauxhall from the Royal College of Art in the great era of Henry Moore: 'Just to raise enough money for a holiday in France. He was the "styling department"—there was nobody else; and he was employed to model future body shapes that could be put into production. He began to enjoy the work— and anyway he hadn't the face to walk out as soon as his piggy-bank was filled. So he stayed, and the styling department's strength was increased to two, since it was a two-man job carving and building the matrices for the full-scale plaster models. . . . Now, 35 years later, David Jones presides, at the age of 57, over the extremely elegant and imposing styling department with a staff of 140. . . .'

Styling Vauxhalls means different things to different people. I remember a Vauxhall Craftsman's Guild Awards dinner when the chief speaker was Mr. Edmund Dell, M.P., then Joint Parliamentary Secretary, Ministry of Technology. After outlining the importance as he saw it of safety and comfort he told his audience how car design ought to stress simplicity. 'I may be untypical,' he said, 'but I don't want my car to be a baroque battleship which takes me hours to clean. I haven't the time for that, nor the desire. I polished enough brass in the Army not to want to start polishing chrome. I know that many people think of their cars very affectionately, more affectionately, perhaps, than even a dog. But for me a car is a tool, not a taskmaster nor a plaything. It is a way of getting me from place to place. I don't ask Vauxhall to build a car like this if they think it will not sell: I am not that selfish. I don't want to damage the industry. But it is just possible there may be others like me. . . .'

In December, 1964, I went to see a new landmark in Luton, Vauxhall's new £2½ million Engineering and Styling Centre, built on a 13½ acre site adjoining the main factory. It houses all the Company's 1,700 engineering and styling staff, except those who work at the Vauxhall Research and Test Centre four miles away, the separate engine-test building and at Millbrook. The 86-ft.-high section of this Centre has changed the Luton skyline. Attached to this central block is a two-storey section housing fabrication and test workshops on the ground floor, and workshops, laboratory and the whole of the styling activities on the floor above. In addition, there is a further 43,000 sq. ft. workshop converted from an older structure. Natural amenities of the site have been improved by landscaping and by strengthening the banks of the River Lee which runs through it. It is architecturally striking, to those seeing it for the first time. The 400-ft. south elevation features 750 angled concrete cladding units in deep green and white, giving a textured effect and breaking up the vast expanse of window area. The 40-ft.-high canopy over the main entrance, as impressive as any I have seen in Detroit, is faced with quartzite surfaced underneath with mosaics.

Top executives at this Centre are the Chief Engineer, John Alden, C. Eng., F.I.Mech.E., M.S.A.E., M.I.R.T.E., and the

Director of Styling, David B. Jones, A.R.C.A. Each is at the head of his own team, naturally working in close liaison. Under the Chief Engineer major responsibility is in several main areas such as product design, experimental, research, advanced design and development. These main divisions are themselves divided. Product Design, for instance, is broadly divided into car and commercial-vehicle departments. There is a comparable division of responsibility under David Jones—into such groups as car exteriors, interiors, commercial-vehicle styling, advanced projects and others. Yet another section of the Centre is that of materials procurement. It is responsible for spending over £450,000 (about $1 million) each year on material for proto-type building, plus special equipment for research and experi-mental work.

There is a strict security check in all departments, since industrial espionage is not unknown in the world car industry. However, while there are secret measures to prevent unwanted information from getting *out*, there is also a very extensive information section to ensure that technical information gets *in* to research engineers and stylists. The Centre has its own technical library, with records and books on every conceivable aspect of automobile engineering. Technical journals published in most countries are kept and indexed electronically. The recording of research and test findings and the transfer of huge masses of information used to involve 7 million square feet of drawing paper each year. It is impossible to visualise such an area of paper; in fact it just about covers the floor area of the entire Vauxhall plants at Luton and Ellesmere Port. Now everything is handled by microfilming, using IBM cards and a Rank Xerox in every main centre. Drawings and data are microfilmed, with 25 additional copies for oversea plants.

The Centre also deals with its own printing and records, printing and collating, storing and distributing a vast amount of drawings and data. In the Centre's photographic section every type of drawing, document and chart is photographed.

There is equipment to print full-size body drawings on to sheets of specially prepared sensitized aluminium. There is an automatic document lift serving all four floors of the main Engineering and Styling office block, and everything is speeded with the microfilm technique. Original drawings and other vital records are micro-filmed and stored well away from Luton, in secure underground vaults. Blueprints no longer need to be reproduced by roller-process in a machine handling prints up to 54 in. wide on continuous rolls.

As David Jones' Styling department sees new models taking shape—models due next year, or several years ahead—the security is highest here. This area occupies most of the Centre's first floor, along the north-facing side of the building, so the studios receive neutral north light. Vauxhall's own designers helped to design the styling areas, and to a visitor the ultra-modern décor and the whole 'feel' of the Centre reflect the forward-looking nature of the creative work being done.

'Every single detail of the looks of a car has to be considered,' I was told at the Centre, 'from the shape and position of the instrument switches to the overall shape of the finished vehicle. This work is in two main parts, designing and building full-scale models. The layout of the styling department follows the same division, into studios and workshops. There are six styling studios, each with a special function—three for car exteriors, others for interiors, commercial vehicle cabs, advanced design and body development. Then we have a bigger "appraisal" studio, an auditorium where styling projects can be examined from all angles—not only by the designers but by the Product Policy group which meets at least twice a month.'

At the end of this auditorium where prototype Vauxhalls are seen from every angle, and argued about constructively, is a conference room nicknamed the 'working boardroom'. It is separated from the main viewing area by remote-controlled electrically operated floor-to-ceiling glass screens. A suggestion that this helps the Product Policy group to talk about the new projects without embarassing the designers is probably true! Nevertheless, when the final new Vauxhall outcome reaches the streets, it does have to face critical public observation from every angle, by the Press and engineering trade groping underneath, from observers on bus-tops, and through the wind-screens of other cars which the new model overtakes. This happens at any time of day or night, under all weather and lighting conditions.

At Luton the studios and auditorium not only have a north light but their sloping ceilings are covered with diffused, colour-corrected tube lighting. All six studios and the auditorium open on to an outside viewing terrace 350 ft. long, 70 ft. wide, completely hidden from all other parts of the building to avoid artistic disturbance.

The long corridor dividing the studios from the work-shops takes privileged visitors to the shops where full-sized styling models are built. There is a metal shop, a wood shop, and glass-fibre shop, and a paint and soft-trim shop. From these workshops come the full-scale models (in glass-fibre on wooden framing, and complete with all metal trim) from which future production models may evolve. These are the models which first come under critical examination in the auditorium and on the private viewing terrace.

All told, some 2,000 men and women are on the staff of the Centre, together with Chaul End research laboratory, and some of them have an extraordinarily interesting job in what Luton calls 'Fabrication'. This is virtually a miniature factory within a factory. Here they produce complete prototype vehicles *in running order*.

'Up to thirty experimental vehicles may be built in a year,' they told me, 'each one costing as much as £30,000. Naturally not all the design ideas built into these prototypes reach the point of actual production.'

In contrast to the main Luton and Ellesmere Port factories where much engine production is semi-automated, everything in Fabrication is hand-built. The Centre's machine shop is capable of turning out all the components of an engine, while allied to this engine-shop are other workshops to produce the rest of the prototype car or truck—sheet-metal-shop, trim-shop, paint-shop and pattern-shop. New materials and methods are continually being tried. For example, traditional hardwoods are giving way to new plastic materials for patterns and models.

This Fabrication section is one of the very few places in the world where a completely new prototype car is first built by hand. And then it is quite possible the project will be scrapped and not go forward into production in future years. To the layman, much of this build-up work looks rather like testing and measuring: for instance, in the main machine shop many experimental engine components are made up using initially what is known as a jig-borer, a large green-enamelled precision boring machine which can work in many planes. The blue-enamelled bed has micro-optical aids to give very precise settings. To reduce unnecessary time taken by hand processes, all main systems and tools in this section have colour-coded parts. In the wood-shop the first wooden models and mock-ups are built—not necessarily complete cars, of course, but details such as body panels, front or rear sections, roof sections or facia panels. In the sheet-metal-shop a huge Schuler 'stretch' press is used to shape experimental body panels, while smaller presses reduce the amount of hand panel-beating.

In the next chapter we shall see how Vauxhalls are tested at the new £3½ million 700-acre proving ground, but, of course, bench-testing—engineers prefer to call it rig-testing—of certain components is every bit as important as the continuous road-test programmes of the development engineers. In fact, rig-testing offers some advantages over road work. It is possible on the workshop test rigs to multiply certain tests hundreds of times, and to control and record them with great accuracy. This helps determine life-probability of a component, and its behaviour can be studied under very prolonged usage. For

Above. Experimental Vauxhall, the prototype two-seater XVR, constructed in 1966 as a design and styling exercise.

Below. Brabham Viva, the 90 and SL 90 models of which were continued throughout 1967 and 1968 without change. This view shows twin 150 CD carburetters, new inlet manifold. Big-bore straight-through exhaust is here partly concealed by the battery.

Above. Victor 2000 at Elsinore shipyard, Denmark. Early in 1968 this model was awarded the Don Safety Trophy as the vehicle making the greatest contribution to road safety during the preceding year.
Below Full-width bonnet giving all-round access to the Victor introduced in 1967 in 1·6- and 2-litre form, with belt-driven overhead camshaft. Toothed belt can be seen here.

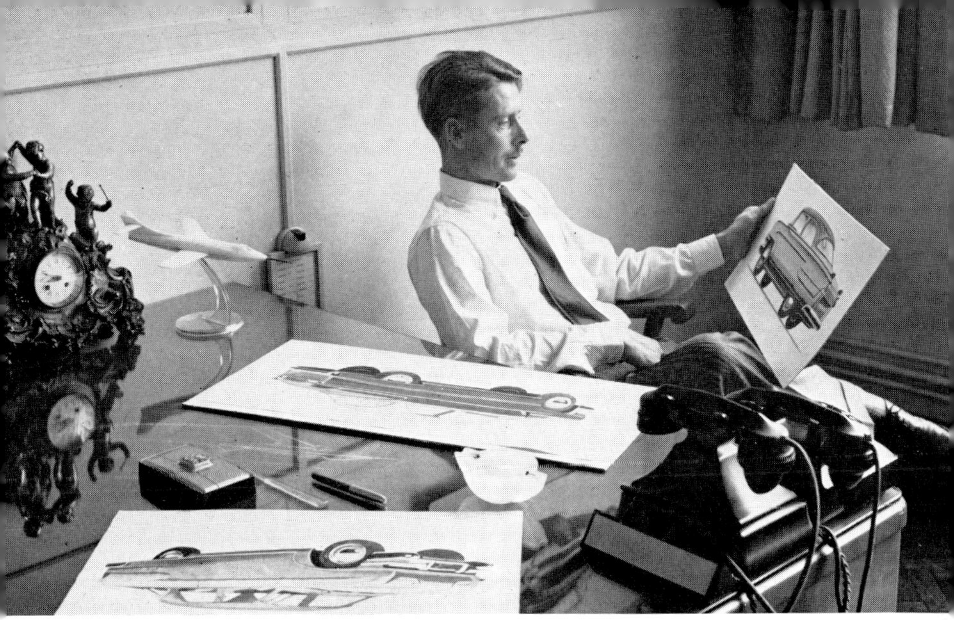

Above. Vauxhall's Styling Director, David Jones. His first complete design was a coupé based on the Ten of 1938, before which he had a further five years' experience as a Vauxhall stylist.
Below. GM's vice-president of styling, William L. Mitchell, sees progress of an experimental GM-X as it takes shape in clay.

Above. Here, gathered at GM's Technical Center in 1957, for the Corporation's 50th year, are 29 of the great GM team led by Alfred P. Sloan Jnr. (president for over 40 years) which built GM from a group of ineffectual companies into the biggest industrial organisation in the world.
Below. Vauxhall Motors' $13\frac{1}{2}$-acre Engineering Centre at Luton.

example, in this test section is a bench with a battery of a dozen complete electrical units (headlamps, direction indicators, stop lights and so forth), with recording instruments showing the number of times the units can be switched on and off before bulbs fail or other faults introduced by changing temperature of contacts.

Similar devices record the number of times a spring can be fully flexed before failure, how long a switch will last, how much compressing a seat can take and still hold its shape, how many wipes a screen-wiper can provide, and so on. In addition to these bench tests, there is a fleet averaging 280 vehicles and the findings and recommendations of engineers working with this fleet are reported to the design engineers.

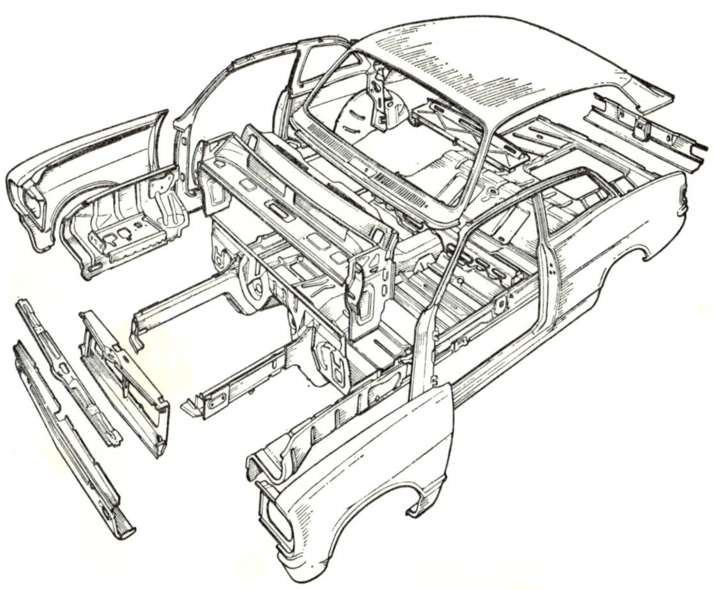

Design features of the integral body construction of the Viva, as first introduced during 1967. One-piece pressings are used for roof and windscreen. Swagings and reinforcements help to avoid body resonance.

All this contributes to Vauxhall's integrity, but it would be foolish to suppose that *on the whole* people are less influenced by reputation and the recommendation of other motorists than they are in their own assessment of what they see. 'Styling' in the broadest sense—including engineering innovation and development—is primarily what makes up the customer's mind.

This was clarified for me in 1962 by William Swallow, then Vauxhall Chairman and Managing director, at a time when the new Victor Estate car and the VX4/90 were introduced.

'It is all too easy if you are in the business of big-scale manufacturing,' he said, 'to let the word "standardisation" become the keystone of your marketing policy. It is true you cannot make cars to individual measure and still sell them at good enough prices to stay in big-time business. But you can—and in my view you must—remember that you are selling to individuals; that you are not selling brooms or pots of meat paste, or anything else in which uniformity is no deterrent; you are selling individual pleasure or individual purpose to individual families or individual firms.

'The way we have gone about this at Vauxhall has led—in little more than five years—to the doubling of the number of basic models offered, and to ever-widening ranges of colour options and treatments. We have moved a long way since the "any-colour-so-long-as-it's-black" days, and from the time when the only answer to individual ideas on equipment was whatever compromise you could find in the accessory shops.

'Vauxhall became familiar very early with the latent demand that existed for dual-purpose vehicles, through the popularity of conversions of our Bedford light vans. Martin Walter's Dormobile is just one example of the variations on the dual-purpose theme that clearly showed the wish of many people for transport designed to take passengers or perambulators, potatoes or playthings. As soon as we had ready a model that could be built as saloon or estate car without too much increase in tooling costs, an estate car went into factory production. That was the first Victor estate. It gained a strong following. We were so encouraged by its success that when we saw the good-looking successor to it that David Jones had designed as part of the new Victor range we decided to base its price on the belief that a really low figure would justify itself by the demand —and thereby the production volume—it created. We have in fact sold as many as we had capacity to make, and could have sold more. . . .

'The concept of the VX4/90 evolved against a different background, though one with common factors. A number of buyers had indicated a preference for a medium-sized saloon with a higher-than-average performance, yet retaining the cost advantages of volume-produced basic structure and parts. In the Victor we felt we had a car that would take this kind of development. If we could use the basic body and a high-proportion of the parts; lift performance appreciably and modify road-holding and braking to match; build in an appropriate level of comfort, instrumentation and so on; if we could do these things and hold the basic price down to the £600–£700 bracket we felt we would have a car that would bring a new group of drivers into our fold.

'We scheduled to build about a thousand a month. In fact we had to build more. We started production in late January, 1962, and on 7th September we had built the 10,000th. No fewer than 3,500 had gone overseas, to 80 countries. . . .' (This model was so popular that, although temporarily dropped in 1967, it was reintroduced in modified form in 1969.)

'More than ever before, as time passes, the motor manufacturer who wants to stay in business will have to broaden his field of forward vision, so that he can anticipate the needs of the ever-increasing number of motorists who want their cars tailored closely to their own ideas.'

This was nearly a decade ago, and now the importance of forward styling is more obvious than ever. For this reason, the Vauxhall investment of £2½ million in the Engineering and Styling Centre is in the long-term interests of future genera-tions of Vauxhall drivers. It is a symbol of the future.

The Centre has three symbols of its own. When you walk the ultra-modern corridors after being given your pass and put into the care of a Luton official, you can hardly fail to be impressed by a large high-relief of the Vauxhall heraldic emblem (a reminder of the griffin of Fulk le Breant) cast in glass-fibre and copper-plated. This is by styling director David Jones. At the end of the central corridor is a large suspended mobile of sheet brass, by Hamish Macpherson, A.R.B.S., a senior Vauxhall designer. And forming a 'window' to the rear wall of the auditorium where prototype Vauxhalls are viewed is an eight-foot-diameter concrete sculpture inset with thick stained glass, the work of Vauxhall's executive designer Brian Adcock, Des.R.C.A.

Appropriately, it is based on an abstraction of two themes, the wheel and the nucleus.

IO

Punishment Park

In the heart of Bedfordshire, within a few miles of the Luton and Dunstable plants, is Vauxhall's research centre, Chaul End. On this 58-acre site there are facilities for advanced laboratory and field research and for track-testing; this latter facility is now superseded by the 700-acre 'punishment park' at Millbrook, 22 miles north of Luton.

Why is it necessary to retain two establishments? Reason for continuing use of the Chaul End proving ground is that here are located many specialist facilities such as the strain-testing laboratories and the first radio-isotope centre to be set up in Britain exclusively devoted to automobile research.

Explains John H. Alden, Director and Chief Engineer: 'In the organisation of the Engineering Department, the Chaul End Research laboratories come within the responsibility of the manager of the research and development group. A proportion of the work carried out is related to advanced projects, but because of their specialised knowledge and equipment members of the group render an extended development service to the engineering department as a whole, and indeed at times to the whole Vauxhall organisation. Facilities available in the laboratories have been continuously developed and enlarged. Even basically familiar services such as measurements using strain gauges have lost many of their old limitations. . . .'

While the average Vauxhall owner on a factory visit does not have an opportunity of seeing the laboratory processes at Chaul End, John Alden's team do not need to concern themselves

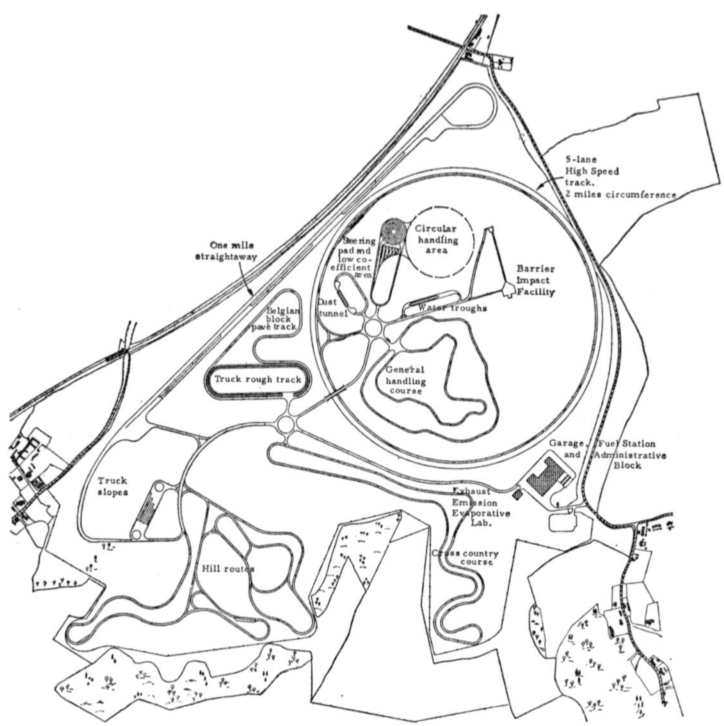

Layout of the proving ground at Millbrook, Bedfordshire. This Vauxhall site is 700 acres in area, with difference of levels of 250 feet between the high-speed circuit and the highest point on the hill routes.

with any thought of industrial espionage. There is, in fact, regular disclosure of much information from Chaul End, especially in the technical publications of professional bodies such as the Automobile Division of the Institution of Mechanical Engineers. This follows the trend set by Maurice Platt, M.Eng, M.S.A.E., Vauxhall's Chief Engineer from 1953 until 1963, who published many papers particularly relating to safety measures in car design. Platt's information relayed to other automotive engineers was not confined to Vauxhall nor even to General Motors engineering, but to the Road Research Laboratory, to the MIRA (Motor Industry Research Association) track and laboratory, and even to the work done by rival car manufacturers such as Chrysler who set up an 'Impact-simulation' laboratory. The first in Europe is at Vauxhall's Safety Laboratory at Millbrook.

Sections of Chaul End today are occupied with hydraulic vibrator tests, electromagnetic vibrators, roller tests, vibration and noise-analysis tests, automatic graph-plotting, analog-computing, the Stresscoat technique, strain-gauge applications, radiography, and wear measurement by radio isotopes. Most of these sections are white-tiled or with decor similar to that of an operating theatre, brilliantly lit with fluorescent strip lamps since much of the work must go on day and night. The following description of work in each section is based on John H. Alden's notes.

At first glance to a layman, the hydraulic vibrator equipment resembles a particularly well-equipped garage servicing pit, with an inbuilt lifting jack of giant proportions. It is in fact a ram unit to which oil is fed at pressures up to 3,000 psi directed to either end of the ram via fast-acting valves, servo-controlled so that the position of the ram at any instant can be governed by feeding a suitable voltage to the servo. Generally this voltage feed is a sine-wave in the frequency range of DC (zero) to 30 cycles per second, which, of course, is in the musical bass-note band. A thrust of over 4,000 lb is available, with a maximum stroke of 9 in. from end to end. Part of the available thrust can be used as a steady pre-load. Thrust and stroke available diminish as the frequency is increased. The upper limit for many practical purposes appears to be 30 cps, although the ram will respond at frequencies up to several hundred cycles per second at very small amplitudes.

'It is used,' explain the research engineers, 'to investigate ride-frequency characteristics of vehicles, to study seat-vibration characteristics, and to establish the dynamic and static stiffness of rubber units such as engine mounts; also we can use it for certain fatigue tests for which the mechanical or electro-magnetic shakers are not suitable.'

A complete assembly such as an engine or a transmission system can be mounted on an electro-magnetic shaker. Giant electric armatures oscillate frameworks on which are bolted parts to be tested. Chaul End's electro-magnetic shakers generate vibrating forces with frequencies ranging from 5 to 2,000 cps, with maximum thrust ranging between ± 250 lb and ± 700 lb. At low frequencies it is possible to achieve maximum amplitude of the shaker spindle of about one inch overall or, in engineering terms, ± 0.5 in. Each shaker is powered by an alternating current of variable frequency and amplitude, provided by one of five 1-kW amplifiers controlled from electronic oscillators or other signal sources. Noise and vibration paths through large units such as engines or transmission systems can be plotted with the aid of this equipment, or equally one small single component can be shaken and observed for hours or weeks.

'Typical of the research for which these electro-magnetic vibrators are used,' the engineers explain, 'is the investigation of the sensitivity of vehicles or components to an unbalanced condition of rotating parts. Another area of use is for checking the fatigue-strength of all sorts of components from crankshafts and fans to mirror arms. With this equipment we can also plot the noise and vibration paths through engines, transmissions and body structures. In conjunction with vibration-measuring equipment we can investigate what are termed vibration modes. In the old days, for example, many engines were said to have a vibration period at certain rev-rates. Nowadays, where the vibration mode of a car component is well defined and the frequency is fairly low—say between 30 and 300 cps—we can use stroboscopes to make the deflections of the component or struxture visible in slow-motion.'

Most motorists are familiar with roller testing if they have ever had the car's brakes tested at one of the many service stations where the vehicle can be 'driven' standing still, the road-wheels simply rotating large rollers built into underground pits. At Chaul End the equipment is not used for this purpose, of course. It is much more elaborate and sophisticated. There is a series of brilliantly lit pits over which a car is driven, fixed in position so that the driving wheels are on the rollers, then the throttle can be opened to give the equivalent of up to 125 mph.

A varying degree of braking torque is applied by means of a water brake, and this is sufficient to hold the test vehicle's top-gear speed down to about 25 mph for a Viva, and to 45 mph on a 3·3 litre Cresta. Much bigger vehicles can be tested on the rollers, to a maximum axle-load of 2,500 lb. At full throttle the maximum power absorption is 300 bhp. Naturally an engine would tend to run hot at full power, since although the road-wheels may be registering 80 or 90 mph through the rollers, the car is really stationary. This minor problem is overcome by having a sliding platform supported across the pit in front of the car: on it is mounted a large fan driven by a 3 hp motor supplementing the cooling provided by the vehicle's own engine fan.

Why do the engineers roller-test a car? 'Chief use of the test,' they explain, 'is in measuring levels of noise and vibration in engines, axles and drive-lines. Other applications include evaluation of transmission efficiencies, and measurement of exhaust back-pressure effects. It has several important advantages over the conventional on-the-road test, because conditions in the laboratory workshop can be repeated at will, and obviously can be closely controlled. Indoor testing is unaffected by weather or traffic conditions. Moreover, roller testing eliminates random vibrations from road surfaces, which are unavoidable in normal road-testing.'

It is frequently possible exactly and immediately to locate the source of a vibration, noise or vehicle-ride peculiarity.

I

However, in most cases each possible cause of noise or vibration
has its own characteristic frequency; thus if the various frequencies created by a vibration are measured, the area of investigation can be considerably reduced. At times one can
even pin-point the source of noise or vibration in this way.
Even if the root cause of the trouble is known, further test
work can be speeded by making scientific records of the effects
of certain specific changes, as opposed to relying on individual
and often subjective impressions.

Accelerometers and microphones operate by detecting the
vibrations at a particular point in a structure, or in the air
around it, and then producing an electrical voltage that is
directly proportional to these vibrations. Standard amplifiers,
analysers and recording instruments are then used to interpret
what is happening in the original vibration.

Typical of this type of test is a seven-channel instrument
recording vibration or noise signals from seven different
points in a car simultaneously. This equipment is portable.
I saw it in use recording the ride vibrations in the floor of a
vehicle. The electrical signal from the accelerometer pick-up
was being recorded on instrumentation-type magnetic tape
which, after several test runs, is played back in the laboratory
into frequency-analysing equipment. This in turn operates a
graph-plotter giving the frequency spectrum of the original
vibration.

Data-type tape machines indicate the increased use of
tape-recording and analysing techniques, and the seven-
channel system allows rapid comparisons to be made of what
is happening at all these points at any given moment. Basic
diagnostics techniques are the same no matter what the vibration spectrum may be, and the Chaul End engineers have
rapid techniques for detecting such things as a 'boom' period
in a car body.

I suppose no major technical area these days is complete
without its computer, and Chaul End is no exception.

In car-engineering research the computer provides a convenient way of simulating the behaviour of various vehicle systems, provided that the relevant characteristics involved can be expressed as equations.

These equations are set up so that voltages at various points in the computer system behave in a fashion identical with the physical variables in the actual system. These voltages are then plotted on convenient scales as if they were actual measurements taken on a vehicle.

'Applications on the Chaul End analog computer are varied,' they will tell you. 'It is used, for instance, to establish optimum braking distribution for cars, trucks and articulated vehicles, including applications for load-sensing and "g". Using this computer it is also possible for us to predict the degree of load-transfer from wheel to wheel during cornering.

'The analog computer can deal with investigations where non-linear springs, backlash or friction are involved. It lends itself readily to the solution of design problems where a particular characteristic is to be optimised but many variables have to be taken into account. A computer drastically reduces the amount of experimental work needed on prototype Vauxhalls or systems.'

Vauxhall's computer data centre uses IBM 360's for commercial work and production planning. However, Chaul End's smaller independent computer has its own special advantages for initial investigation of problems that are not too clearly understood at that stage, and where an ultra-high degree of accuracy is not required. Vauxhall's analog computer has fifty-five operational amplifiers, and also available are 'function generators' and multipliers, plus various types of read-out equipment such as a six-channel UV galvanometer chart recorder, a graph-plotter and a four-beam-display oscilloscope.

Nominal computing accuracy on summing and integration is

0·1 per cent, giving an overall accuracy in results of 5–10 per cent. Naturally the degree of accuracy depends to an extent on the complexity of the problem, on the assumptions made in formulating the equations, and on the accuracy of the data fed into the computer. In the past, whenever an engineer wished to plot a graph to understand trends in results, or to demonstrate results for a technical report, he had to draw the curves manually. Now, facilities exist at Chaul End in which the pen tracing the lines of the graph can be controlled automatically by electrical signals, instead of by hand.

The analog computer can predict what the motions of various parts of a car will be when driving over a bump. An electronic graph-plotter is operated from the computer and puts the results into visual form. The plotter can also be coupled to vibration-analysing equipment, to plot the variations in vibration that occur when the speed or test frequencies are changed. Alternatively, a keyboard can be attached to the plotter and the points on the graph typed-in directly from the X and Y co-ordinates. This method is used at Vauxhall to plot curves from figures produced by their digital computers in other buildings.

Some valuable work is being done at Chaul End laboratories with what is known to scientists and physicists as the Stresscoat technique.

An important property of the specialised Stresscoat lacquer is that it becomes brittle after being sprayed on to a surface. From this it follows that it can have important uses for a research team investigating the stresses present in car and van bodies, truck cabs, road-wheels, suspension components, clutch-housings, gearboxes and so on. Even engine pistons can be Stresscoat tested on a rig. When Stresscoat lacquer is applied to parts of a vehicle, the strains set up under normal operating conditions are usually enough to produce distinctive patterns of fine cracks in the lacquer where concentrated tensile stress occurs.

Spraying and drying are done in a specially adapted room

into which vehicles up to 28 ft. in length can be driven. The material costs about £7 a quart, and the Chaul End operatives applying it wear outfits with helmets reminiscent of Moon-walking astronauts.

What at first seems quite a simple technique has been brought to a highly sophisticated art at Vauxhall. They tell you: 'The level of the stress at which the lacquer coating begins to crack can be found by calibrating specimens. So the crack patterns not only indicate areas of high stress and the direction of it, but also give an indication of the degree of stress involved.

'Lacquer can be used over large areas, and experience has indicated to us a very close relationship between the stress indications revealed by crack-patterns and the fatigue failures resulting from pavé and rough-track testing. Stresscoat testing has an advantage in that preliminary results from a test are normally available within twenty-four hours of the lacquer being sprayed on, whereas track-testing to get the same result may take days or even weeks. If a component can be tested in a rig, so that the imposed load is accurately controlled, stresses produced can be determined to an accuracy of 10 per cent or better. When the part is to be tested under actual operating conditions it is normal practice to use Stresscoat to reveal the overall stress pattern, and then to repeat the test using strain gauges to measure the strain values more accurately. And when stresses due to compression are being investigated, we have to use different methods—they involve the use of test rigs to produce the required load.'

There are limits, and Chaul End has found that the Stress-coat process is not suitable where significant temperature-changes occur in the part under test, or where the ambient temperature is greater than some 30° C. Nor can they use this lacquer where oil or grease are present. That is why strain-gauge tests must be made to investigate dynamic stresses more fully.

Vauxhall research engineers apply strain-gauge techniques

to measure stresses in structural sections and in road-wheels, to measure the operating torque in rear-axle half-shafts, to discover the loads imposed on suspension linkage members, to record oil-pressure fluctuations in an engine, to measure the fore-and-aft movements of suspension arms under operating conditions, and for a score of other tests. Basically a strain gauge consists of a continuous grid or zigzag of fine wire bonded to the component under test. The size of this grid may vary between about $\frac{1}{16}$in. square to nearly 1-sq. in. When the component is subjected to its operating stress, the very minute mechanical strains of the metal surface under the gauge cause a corresponding change in the dimensions of the grid, and so also in the electrical resistance of the wire. This change is detected and used to operate a pen recorder of a galvanometer chart recorder. Deflections of the pen or the galvanometer 'trace' can be calibrated to indicate stress or strains in the metal.

'A strain guage indicates the average strain over an area,' the research engineers explain, '*and in the direction in which the strain is imposed*. This means some prior information is needed to determine the most suitable place for the gauge itself. The Stresscoat system usually gives us this information.'

Permanent chart records can be produced for vibratory stresses of a frequency of up to 250 cps without having to use a photographic darkroom. This frequency-ceiling covers virtually all normal vehicle operating conditions excluding those related to engines. For engine components in motion, the stress signals can be shown on an oscilloscope and photographed in a technique such as that employing cameras with Polaroid Land backs and Polascope film at speeds up to 10,000 ASA equivalent.

'With modern adhesives,' the research men explain, 'strain gauges can be applied direct to the vehicle and are ready for actual testing within the hour, no heat being needed to get rapid setting. Strain gauges can be used, with suitable precautions, in oil or water. Those normally used in this laboratory can be operated in temperatures up to 100° C, but there are alternative systems and wiring methods available to us.'

Additional virtues of strain gauges include their value in making up what are termed 'load-cells', displacement indicators and pressure-indicators. Recorded traces can be calibrated directly if necessary by applying loads, deflections and so forth to the cell. Amplifier systems and galvanometer recorders will handle signals from six separate gauges simultaneously, so that the amplitude and relative sequence of events at several points can be compared.

Making wear measurements by radio-isotopes is one of the most up-to-date techniques at Vauxhall. As they explain, when any material, solid or liquid, is put into an atomic pile and bombarded with neutrons it becomes radioactive (meaning that it gives off radiation spontaneously), and this is a radio-isotope. Radiation from it can be measured, as no doubt every science-fiction schoolboy knows, and this process is called 'counting'. The more radioactive the material put in front of a detector, the higher the 'count-rate'. This relationship is the basis of wear measurement, since, of course, the radio-isotope can be induced to go into places which no other measuring device can easily reach.

'The use of radio-isotopes to measure wear in vehicle parts is based on this simple principle,' the engineers say. 'The part to be tested for wear-rate is usually running in oil which is in continuous circulation—cylinder liners, for instance, or axle gears and roller-bearings. If the part is made radioactive by irradiating it in an atomic pile, then the material worn off the part by wear accumulates in the oil. Since this "wear debris" is itself radioactive, the level of radioactivity in the oil is a measure of the wear that has occurred in the part. It is a simple matter to drain off samples of oil during test running, and to measure the level of radioactivity.'

Counting equipment is highly sensitive, and under favourable conditions wear can be measured after a few minutes or even seconds of operation. This can be extended to produce charts of wear over thousands of miles, given suitable isotopes. Sensitivity of this method is far greater than that possible with weighing, or with physical measurements; and it is a big advantage at Chaul End that the comparative brevity of each test makes it practicable to study the effects of many *more* test conditions than would otherwise be possible. One limiting factor can be the 'mileage' (time factor) required to run-in a component for each new test, so that a true reading of normal operating wear is obtained.

Not every component to be tested is run in oil, so it may be asked how the research engineers use radio-isotopes then.

They explain: 'In circumstances where "wear debris" cannot be collected in the circulating oil or other fluid, it may be possible to treat a local area of the wearing part with radio-active material, and then measure the reduction in the radio-activity of this area as wear takes place. This is the technique used here at one time to measure wear in tyres.

'Effects of altering front-wheel camber-angle and toe-in have been investigated with isotopes. Each test-run on a tyre involved some 110 miles of running-in, and 55 miles for the actual measurement. Another application of the radio-isotope process is to the measurement of wear in gearbox synchromesh cones. These basic techniques have other applications . . . for example, we can measure engine-oil consumption by adding a radioactive tracer to the oil, then measuring the level of radio-activity in the exhaust gas.'

When parts have been activated in an atomic pile, the rays given off are dangerous, as everyone knows. Since effectiveness of these rays falls off considerably with distance, assembling these radioactive parts into a vehicle or rig is done remotely, by mechanical hands, tongs and grabs similar to those seen in science documentaries dealing with laboratory and medical applications of isotopes. Of course, this is not entirely the end of the matter, for when activated parts are brought back from an atomic centre it may be necessary to store them for some time until particular sections of a test can be continued.

For safety, at some distance from the Chaul End laboratory are 'wells' sunk several feet deep, into which radioactive parts are placed. The shielding effect of the earth and concrete effectively stops the rays.

After the white-coated, scientific atmosphere of Chaul End it is an exciting contrast to drive a Vauxhall twenty-two miles to Millbrook, perhaps the toughest proving-ground in Europe. The first stage of this 'punishment park' went into operation late in 1969, and will be completed after the first edition of this *Vauxhall Companion* goes to press.

'It's no kid's playground,' they boast at Millbrook. 'We really put the boot in.'

There is a circular high-speed track, five lanes wide . . . a mile-long circuit of Belgian pavé, with king-size potholes. Uneven granite blocks are set in concrete. The average test is 1,200 miles on this circuit—then the prototypes are stripped for critical examination.

Two tracks each 300 ft. long contain fresh and salt water. Salt spray comes in from the sides, simulating the worst of winter slush. There are 180° curves with treacherous camber, test-hills with gradients worse than 1-in-4 for stop, re-start and acceleration tests. There is a straight four-lane mile of level asphalt, with entry speeds of up to 100 mph, and alongside this are noise- and vibration-generating surfaces like washboard and broken concrete. A steering test area checks a car's handling on a wide variety of wet and dry surfaces, showing how a vehicle can stand up to side stresses, centrifugal forces, and roll-angles. There is a dust-tunnel, and a 75-ton concrete block for head-on impact tests . . . electronically remote-controlled.

Vauxhall's slogan since Millbrook was opened is: 'If a test vehicle can't take Punishment Park you can't buy the finished article.'

Velox to Ventora

Former Vauxhall chairman Bill Swallow, quoted in Chapter 9 on the importance of having a wide range of cars to please the greatest number of people, said: 'The way we have gone about this at Vauxhall has led—in little more than five years—to the doubling of the number of basic models offered.' That was in 1962, and the range from the original Velox (the name under which the historic sporting 30/98 was introduced in pre-war years) to the present Viva, Victor, Ventora, Cresta and Viscount reads like a computer programme.

At Luton they have found it is becoming difficult to drop a model. The VX 4/90 was introduced for the reasons Bill Swallow outlines, and was temporarily put out of production in 1967, but demand brought a new, high-performance VX 4/90 back in October, 1969, and it was shown at the Paris Motor Show.

Popularity of many models through the years has caused some type-names to be perpetuated in a multitude of series, and to clarify the picture (especially for owners of old Vauxhalls wanting to verify the precise model to discover a trade-in 'book' value) it is instructive to start at the year 1948, in the summer of which the first models of this post-war era appeared. These were the L-type Velox and Wyvern, and in 1948–51 they were the only Vauxhall models produced. In retrospect the styling appears to bridge the gap between the immediate pre-war appearance of the H and J-types and the complete breakaway in Vauxhall line which appeared in mid-1951. These L-type models were the first Vauxhalls to have a steering-column gear-shift. The

Velox had a 2¼-litre engine, six cylinders, while the four-cylinder 1½-litre Wyvern was almost identical in outward appearance but had the added charm (since petrol was already becoming more costly) of giving up to 35 mpg.

Next, from 1951 to 1957, came the E-type models. The 2¼-litre six-cylinder Velox and the 1½-litre Wyvern brought in curved windscreens and side-opening bonnets. In 1952 a new 'square' (shorter stroke) engine was introduced for both models, 2,262 cc and 1,507 cc. respectively. The year 1953 was Vauxhalls Golden Jubilee, and a number of detail styling changes were made in the cars; a higher-compression head (7·6:1) was an option. The first Cresta appeared in 1954, a super-luxury version of the Velox. Final styling changes including modified grille were made in 1956. It was during the life of the E-type that Vauxhall Motors' output in 1953 topped 100,000 vehicles a year for the first time, and the company produced its millionth vehicle, a happy Jubilee Year. The final E-type Cresta came out in 1957, the year which saw the introduction of another new model, the Victor.

This proved an enormous selling success at home and over-overseas; 390,745 F-type Victors were built, and it quickly became Britain's No. 1 export car. Victor and Victor Super 1½-litre models were launched in February, 1957, and the following year came a two-pedal variant with Newtondrive clutchless gear-shift. This was virtually the first Vauxhall progression towards automatic transmission. The first Victor Estate car was produced in 1958 (Britain's first volume-production factory-built multi-purpose car), and this year saw the 100,000th Victor built, just over fifteen months since the introduction. It was so acceptable to the motoring public that only few changes needed to be made; the Series 2 Victor with a somewhat simplified and cleaner styling was produced for 1959, and through to 1961 other changes were minor, such as a redesigned grille and larger rear windows.

Turning the production clock back for a moment to 1957,

two new handsome six-cylinder models had then been introduced, the PA-type Velox and Cresta, with 2¼-litre over-square engines; they found a ready market, and between 1957 and 1962 173,604 were produced.

This was the beginning of the end for the traditional Vauxhall flutes, the introduction of which was dealt with in Chapter 2. On the 1957–8 PA's flutes were still incorporated on the body sides, as it would have been virtually impossible to use this styling with the flatter bonnet top: by 1959 they had gone completely after 53 years as a Vauxhall styling feature.

Reminiscing about these models of the '50's, a Luton executive said to me with justifiable pride: 'The long-and-low look of the PA-series found immediate favour; it still looks good even today.' This is true. These well-built jobs have lasted, too. For reasons hard to fathom, black was a popular colour during that era, and the outcome is that on the low-price-bracket used-car market one will finds a high proportion of well-preserved elderly Vauxhalls in 'any-colour-so-long-as-it's-black'. A respected friend of mine in the judiciary has a certain prejudice against them, believes that they now largely fall into the hands of impecunious, reckless drivers, so whenever a careless-driving case comes into his court he scans the charge-sheet. 'Ah,' he will venture on occasions, 'I'll wager the defendant was driving an old black Vauxhall.'

It is really a tribute to the marque for having certain long-lasting qualities, and a styling which stayed in popular acceptance for a decade.

In February, 1959, the two millionth vehicle was built by Vauxhall, and it happened to be a PA Cresta. This was the year of introduction of the curved grille, and a one-piece rear window curved round the corners. The Friary estate car was produced, approved by Vauxhall, in Velox and Cresta forms. During 1960 came a new 2½-litre square engine, and Hydra-matic automatic transmission. (See Chapter 12.) By 1962 disc front brakes were an option for the Velox and Cresta, as were separate front seats, and as if to reinforce the long-lasting qualities coupled with traditional Vauxhall reliability, in March, 1962, the warranty cover on all Vauxhalls was increased to twelve months.

A modern styling was introduced in 1961 for the attractive FB-series Victor in a range of four models, and the public was given the first of the VX 4/90's which Bill Swallow described in Chapter 9. In its day the variant gave 44 per cent greater power, with a twin-carburetter 81·6 hp engine of 9·3:1 compression ratio. In turn, the 1964 model announced at the 1963 International Motor Show gave 85·5 gross bhp and over 90 mph maximum. The standard Victor engine went up in size to 1,594 cc, with 69 gross bhp and 8·5:1, and by 1963 disc brakes became an option on the Victor, and standard on the VX 4/90.

Resulting from the wide acceptance of the FB Victor styling, few visible changes were made during the model's life. The only major mechanical change was the increase in engine size for 1963–4 from 1,508 to 1,594 cc. It was a very successful car, and 328,642 were made.

The years 1962–5 were of steady continuing development, since behind the scenes there was a most important growth of Vauxhall production facilities. Building started on the Ellesmere Port site in 1961. This represented a £66 million investment by Vauxhall, aiding the government policy at the time of encouraging growth away from the south-east. Luton heads chose the 393-acre site on Merseyside, built a self-contained car-production plant as modern as any in Europe, and in course of time were to have about 10,000 men and women working there, compared (at the same era) with approximately 18,500 at Luton and 5,700 at the Bedford truck plant and the Vauxhall replacement parts headquarters in Dunstable. Ellesmere Port was tooled up to produce the Viva, born in 1963.

Returning to the larger models, however, the new PB-series Velox and Cresta appeared in 1962, the powerful 2½-litre engine being continued from the PA-series. A three-speed column-change gearbox was standard, and overdrive or Hydramatic transmission were options. Late in 1963 came the Martin Walter estate car on Velox and Cresta: mechanical changes included a lower axle-ratio for the estates, a new 3·3-litre engine and optional four-speed floor-change gearbox. It was an all-time record year for Vauxhall, 1964, when the gratifying total of 342,873 cars and commercial vehicles were sold. PB models continued in production until Motor Show time, 1965, in which year also the Powerglide automatic transmission system replaced Hydramatic.

During these years the general theme of Vauxhall had been 'bigger and better', with ultra-modern styling and smoother, more powerful engines; the sheer magnitude of production (such as the 342,873 total) made it impossible for the Company to cope with the 1-litre class, despite the enormous appeal of the Ten and the 14 hp J-type of the late 1940's. At Ellesmere Port, however, it was possible to concentrate assembly lines on one entirely new series, the Viva.

Two models were introduced at first in this HA series, both two-door saloons, with new-design three-bearing 1,057 cc engines. Compression ratio was 8·5:1, but a 7·3:1 engine was available for areas where only low-grade fuel was available or necessary, and this dropped the peak power by only 6 bhp. Vauxhall rating for the 8·5:1 engine was 44 bhp at 5,200 rpm. A single Solex down-draught carburetter was used, and other mechanical features included a conventional diaphragm spring clutch, four-speed all-synchro box with central change, hypoid bevel final drive, double-wishbones with transverse leaf spring suspension at front, and semi-elliptics at rear, rack-and-pinion steering, Girling drum brakes (8-in.), and optional 8·2-in. front discs with servo. The price steadied to around £527 for the standard HA Viva and £566 for the deluxe model (British domestic prices including purchase tax).

It was a well-deserved marketing success, an entirely new

car from an entirely new Vauxhall factory, a rather more roomy body than others in its class, and a sleek good-looker—partly because the Viva was the first car in Britain to have acrylic lacquer finish. Ellesmere Port worked all around the clock turning out Viva HA's, the 100,000th being built within 10 months of the model's introduction.

An SL version came in the summer of 1965, the '90' models in the autumn—deluxe '90' and SL '90' with 60 bhp engines of 9:1 compression. In time there were five HA models, and by the end of 1965 the 250,000th Viva was built. Ultimately when the HA-series made way for the HB, in March, 1966, no fewer than 307,738 Vivas had been built, and in addition to giving service and pleasure to these many thousands of owners (over half a million now that they are on the used-car market) it is not unimportant to think what prosperity came to Merseyside.

Overlapping this 1-litre-class development, there were many changes in the larger cars. First came the Victor 101, at the London International Motor Show of 1964. These FC-series cars featured that distinctive 'space-curve' look (that is, I believe, a Derek Goatman styling term), with pronounced curvature of the side windows contributing to inside space. Victor 101 models inherited the 1,594 cc engine of the previous $1\frac{1}{2}$ litre range, eventually to be superseded in the autumn of 1967 by the FD Victors. Prior to that, however, two new options were offered in 1965, a limited-slip differential, and Power-glide automatic transmission.

PC Cresta and Cresta deluxe models in October, 1965, marked the disappearance of the model-name Velox. In the new series the 3·3 litre engine gave 140 gross bhp, and options included three-speed column change with or without overdrive, floor change, or Powerglide. The Viscount, a super-luxury variant of the Cresta, was introduced in mid-1966 with Powerglide, powered steering and power-operated windows as standard fitments. David Jones' styling of the black vinyl Viscount roof set an attractive fashion, soon to be flattered by being widely copied by other manufacturers, and the Viscount was certainly Vauxhall's most luxurious car at that time. In 1967 Martin Walter introduced their estate-car conversion of the Cresta Deluxe, giving 60 cu. ft. of space in the rear.

From the Ellesmere Port assembly lines came the HB Viva in 1966. There are comments on certain engineering changes in Chapter 12, but here it may be noted that the engine size was increased from 1,057 to 1,159 cc, and the overall length of the car increased by 6½ in. A new type of all-coil-spring suspension was incorporated in the HB-series. Early in 1967 Vivas were available with Borg Warner automatic transmission, and a Jack Brabham conversion job became available for the '90'. This was offered with twin-carburetters, head and manifold modifications, giving 79 gross bhp. Vauxhall did not supply Brabham-prepared engines as standard, and the conversion was offered by Vauxhall dealers after delivery from the factory.

Brabham conversions proved there are many thousands of Vauxhall enthusiasts anxious to have what has today become known as GT-class performance, nebulous though that label may be since government restrictions in many countries make 'grand touring' a matter of only nostalgic interest. In March, 1968, nevertheless, came the Viva GT, using the 2-litre overhead-camshaft engine similar to that of the new Victor 2000 announced in 1967. This twin-carburetter power unit gives 112 bhp. The GT specification concentrated on safety features and included large disc brakes and full instrumentation. The GT Viva was easily recognised by its matt-black bonnet, twin air scoops and (as Vauxhall Sales Director Geoffrey Moore commented): 'by its fast-disappearing tail-end when one overtakes you!' The 1969/70 GT's were even better.

In June, 1968, two Viva saloons and two estate cars were introduced, these having a 1,600 cc overhead-cam engine giving 83 bhp; and in 1968 a number of four-door saloons were introduced, bringing the total Viva choice to 26 models.

The Diamond Jubilee year of Vauxhall, 1967, was marked by the October launching of two completely new Victors, the FD models Victor and Victor 2000. Here for the first time we had the new overhead-cam four-cylinder engines, 1,599 and 1,975 cc, (83 and 104 bhp respectively), the camshaft drive being by the special toothed belt found so satisfactory in the United States. The system had been primarily researched by General Motors Engineering for the six-cylinder overhead-cam engine of the 1966 Pontiac Motor Division's Tempest.

For the 1967 Victors, Vauxhall's safety energy-absorbing steering-column was standard equipment, and just a few months after the launching the Victor 2000 was awarded the Don Safety Trophy for the vehicle contributing most to road safety during the year. *The Times* called it 'The star of the show' when it was introduced at Earls Court, and the *Sunday Times* rightly dubbed it the 'British car of the year'.

When the VX 4/90 was introduced, at Motor Show time, 1969, it was given the 112 bhp version of the four-cylinder overhead-cam engine previously available only in the Viva GT, and for the rest it incorporated all the Victor's award-winning safety features such as the energy-absorbing column, anti-burst door locks, protrusion-free interior, anti-injury interior mirror, plus certain engineering-specification features of steering and suspension, and the provision of 175/70 HR × 13 radials.

Jerry Ames road-tested the Ventora introduced during 1968–9. He called it 'The best Vauxhall I have driven for years', and *Autocar* confirmed that it has 'the highest performance of any Vauxhall model yet marketed'. Potential Ventora owners should get a back-copy of *Autocar*'s Road Test No. 2175, from which they will see a mean maximum speed of 103 mph, and 0–60 in 11·8 sec. When I tried a Ventora with over 8,000 miles on the clock it was exciting to go from 30 to the legal maximum of 70, using the gearbox sensibly in a shade under 14 sec. Reason for this punchy performance is the

K

incorporation of the 3·3-litre Cresta-type engine in a Victor-type motor-car, giving tremendous torque from low initial engine-revs.

Luton's sales slogan for the Ventora has been 'The Lazy Fireball', giving 'long-striding luxury on the open road, plus lazy top-gear flexibility'. From the engineering viewpoint what matters is the factor of brake-horsepower per ton, and as the initial Ventora engine develops 123 bhp at a fairly 'lazy' 4,600 rpm, pulling a car of kerb weight 23 cwt the factor comes out to some 96·5 bhp per ton laden. On its introduction the Ventora could be had with four-speed all-synchro box, or optionally with overdrive or the two-speed automatic transmission. There have been considerable changes in Vauxhall auto transmissions through the years, as we shall see in the next chapter.

12

Mainly Technical

A two-pedal Victor launched in 1958 used the Newtondrive clutchless gear-shift, and this was the first step towards simplifying gear-changing. Hydramatic automatic transmission became an option two years later, and in 1965 this system was replaced by the Powerglide system.

As there have been marked changes in auto systems, culminating in the GM Automatic three-element torque-converter system adopted for the 1970 Victors and Ventora II, it is useful to look back to Vauxhall's enterprising engineering philosophy when, in October, 1960, they pioneered the way with the Hydramatic—or Hydra-Matic, as purists at first insisted should be the label.

This was primarily developed by the Detroit Transmission Division of GM in association with Vauxhall's British engineering team, for cars of the Cresta/Velox class. The new unit shared the same basic design as the Detroit automatic box, but was lighter, more compact, and from an engineer's standpoint was a very considerable technical achievement. It added only 30 lb to the weight of a manual-change Cresta of Vauxhall, which accounted for the closeness of fuel-consumption figures for cars fitted with both types of drive.

Hydramatic provided three forward ratios and reverse. Top was 1:1 direct, second a reduction of 1·58:1, and first a reduction between 3·03 and 3·64 to 1. Ratios were obtained as in other systems by varying combinations of two epicyclic planetary gear-trains. In low ratio a fluid coupling carried the whole of the drive-load, the small torque-multiplier being responsible for the variation of 3·03 to 3·64. In middle ratio a mechanical multi-plate clutch took the whole load. In top, one-third of the load was taken by the fluid coupling, two-thirds by the mechanical clutch. This arrangement resulted in a smooth, fluid-cushioned start from rest, with the torque-multiplier supplying extra boost for the initial moving-off.

Once the transmission changed into middle ratio the drive was wholly mechanical, and in top the fluid coupling and mechanical clutch share the load as we have just seen. This reduced overall power losses. The fluid coupling was equally efficient on drive and overrun, so the engine was able to give full braking effect when the accelerator foot was lifted.

All ratio changes were made, as in most auto systems, by valves actuated hydraulically according to road speed and throttle opening. First-to-second change took place between 10 and 25 mph, and second-to-third between 15 and 55 mph. There was the usual selector lever with visual indicator on the column for R (reverse), L (low), S (second), D (drive), (N (neutral) and P (park). As is now customary, the starter could be operated only in the neutral and park positions, and a valve was incorporated preventing reverse from coming into action if the forward speed was above 8 mph. In the parked position the road-wheels were locked (but not, of course, in the neutral position), and the L (low) and S (second) positions allowed the retention of low and middle ratios respectively.

In the years following Hydramatic a design team was set up to provide an auto-transmission system even more suitable for European-sized cars. This was a 'task force' of engineers drawn from General Motors in Detroit, from Vauxhall and from GM's other major overseas manufacturing divisions. Backed by the Detroit technical resources, they came up with the system known simply as 'GM Automatic', and to streamline production a manufacturing plant was established in Strasbourg, France. Pro-British protagonists who would have liked to see this box built at Luton were soon convinced by Vauxhall and GM policy that: 'reliability results from high-precision manufacture in a built-for-the-job factory'. As a matter of fact, much Continental European experience, plus extensive development work by Vauxhall engineers at Luton, proved that the new system was indeed most reliable. A Service Training Centre was set up at Luton to implement the new techniques.

Basically this new system consists of a three-element torque converter providing a fluid drive in *all* gears, connected to a box which changes its ratios in response to engine vacuum and road speed. The 'holding' operation of the gear-trains in the box is done by a system of three multi-plate clutches and a brake-band. There is the conventional hydraulic valve bank controlled by engine depression. A novel feature of the transmission's design and manufacture is the use of separate *interchangeable* torque converters, so the unit can be adapted to a range of engine outputs. The transmission body (casing) is common to all, the clutch capacity and hydraulic control system being varied to suit engine power. This is one reason why the system was first introduced for Victors and Ventora II, later becoming an 'automatic' Viva option.

It gives the driver more control over gear-changes and road performance than had been available on any Vauxhall auto-transmission system previously. Without moving the selector from the normal D (drive) position, a driver can select any of the three gear ratios simply by relating accelerator pressure to road-speed. This facility is quite separate from the usual 'kick-down' provision which he can use (as on the Hydramatic and others) for fast acceleration. The floor-mounted selector in the new Vauxhall system has a six-position quadrant instead of the usual five. These are: P (park, positively locking the transmission and preventing the car from rolling either way), R (reverse), N (neutral), D (drive), I (intermediate) and L (low).

In position I the transmission does not allow a change upwards from second gear, so providing downhill engine braking, and on long climbs avoiding constant changes into and out of the top ratio as engine loads vary. Position L holds the transmission in first gear indefinitely, also giving maximum engine braking on steep descents. If a Vauxhall driver wishes, he can start in L and shift to I, and then to D, in much the same way as he would with a manual box, giving a quick getaway. Maintenance needs are simple: a check of oil level every three months, and a brake-band check every two years.

Introduction of the neoprene camshaft-and-auxiliary belt drive is another of those innovations, like the automatic transmission, where it is foolish for a European designer not to accept the experience of Detroit. Nowadays this belt on overhead-camshaft Vauxhall engines is designed to operate without any periodic adjustment in service. Even the jockey-pulley has a sealed ball-bearing. All that it is important to note is that when a high-compression engine is partly dismantled, and the belt has to be removed, the valve-timing mark on the crankshaft pulley needs to be positioned approximately 90° before the top-dead-centre pointer, and while the belt is off the crankshaft must not be rotated through this TDC position as this can cause a foul between pistons and valve heads.

The belt drive is the outcome of research at the General Motors Technical Center, at Warren, Michigan. Different types of sprockets were tried, including aluminium, reinforced phenolic plastic, and cast iron. Ultimately a cast-iron sprocket of a surface-hardened type was found suitable for the crankshaft position. First tests began with a neoprene belt having a high-carbon steel cable as the tension member, but the steel could corrode. A change to stainless steel cords was made, but fatigue failures were apt to show at about 50,000 miles. It chanced that I was invited to the GM Technical Center while tests were being finalised on the timing belt, and indeed after the incorporation of glass-fibre had been approved, durability tests were made for three and a half years at the GM Desert proving ground.

One detail will illustrate technical ingenuity which, unseen, has gone into something as revolutionary as neoprene-belt drive for engine camshafts. On examining a Vauxhall engine with this type of accessory drive, owners may wonder why such a belt does not tend to run off the edge of the sprockets.

Indeed, I asked about this in Detroit, in 1966, and was informed: 'The teeth make positive engagement with the sprockets' axial grooves, and are designed to enter and leave in a rolling manner, much the same as teeth on a gear. The theoretical pitch diameter of each sprocket is slightly larger than the outside diameter, allowing the tension member of the belt to run on the sprockets' theoretical pitch diameter. Sprockets do not have guide flanges for the belt, but (on the Tempest engine) are 0·32 in. wider than the belt.

'Initial test work indicated that this additional width was satisfactory to ensure that the belt would never run off the edges of the sprockets. It was found, however, that the direction of twist of the glass-fibre influenced the direction in which the belt tracks on the sprockets. So we decided to use a dual-twist cord pattern. Here's how it is done. Two continuously wound cords are used, fibres of adjacent cords having a reverse twist. This is all we need to reduce any tendence of the belt to track towards front or rear of the sprockets, and cuts out any need for belt-guides.'

It should be noted that the belt is not made by GM, but by Uniroyal.

As researched by Vauxhall and adapted for the 1969 Victor overhead cam engines, the toothed flexible belt is of neoprene with glass-fibre tension members and nylon tooth facings. It is virtually indestructible, and has been a salient feature of the five-bearing ohc power-unit. Designed nearly eighteen months before a rival engine of the 1,248–1,500 cc type came off the test-bench, and which is neither overhead cam nor crossflow, the Vauxhall unit is fully machined, has hemispherical combustion chambers, large valves arranged for crossflow, double valve springs, four-branch exhaust manifold, and over-square design. In 1,599 cc form it derives 83 bhp gross.

Sports-car enthusiasts are apt to dwell on specification

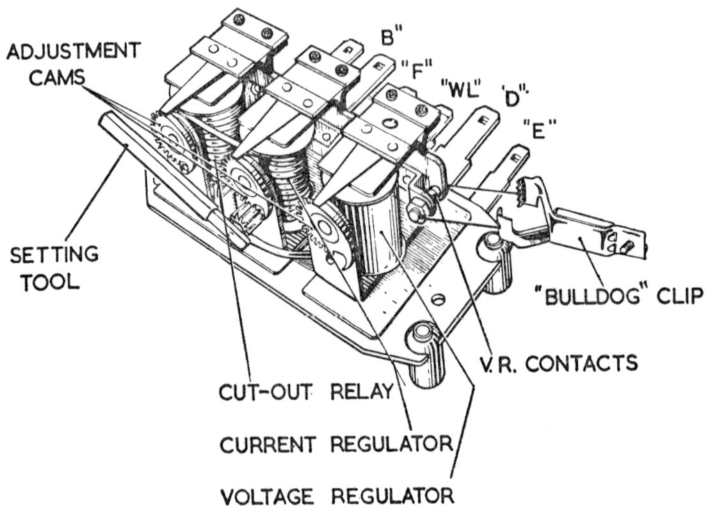

Lucas RB340 current-voltage control unit, which includes temperature compensation, as used on some Vauxhall models having DC generators.

sheets, and to ignore important details. Of course it *is* important that Vauxhall introduced an overhead camshaft unit, but when one looks to past historic engines of this type such as the Bugatti, or to an in-line six still in production it cannot be overlooked that a common problem with them all was tappet adjustment. Vauxhall solved this, in an ohc engine, with a simple Allen-key inserted into a taper-faced adjusting screw. True, the Allen-key was not available to Ettore Bugatti, but Vauxhall design engineers were the first to incorporate the new system and it is a Vauxhall patent.

These are the things for which one must look, and not mere specifications on paper. As a final example, consider the

Viva HB-series introduced in March, 1966. As we have seen, more than 307,000 HA-type Vivas had been sold, and many executives might have believed it was sufficient to introduce new styling gimmicks, or a wider colour range.

John Alden presented me with a specification showing some of the not-obvious changes. 'We laid down a number of basic concepts when we set about designing the new Viva,' he said. 'Drawing on our experience with the original Viva, we naturally wanted to continue with most of its past successful features, and we were determined to design into the car further improved standards of refinement, safety, reliability. . . .'

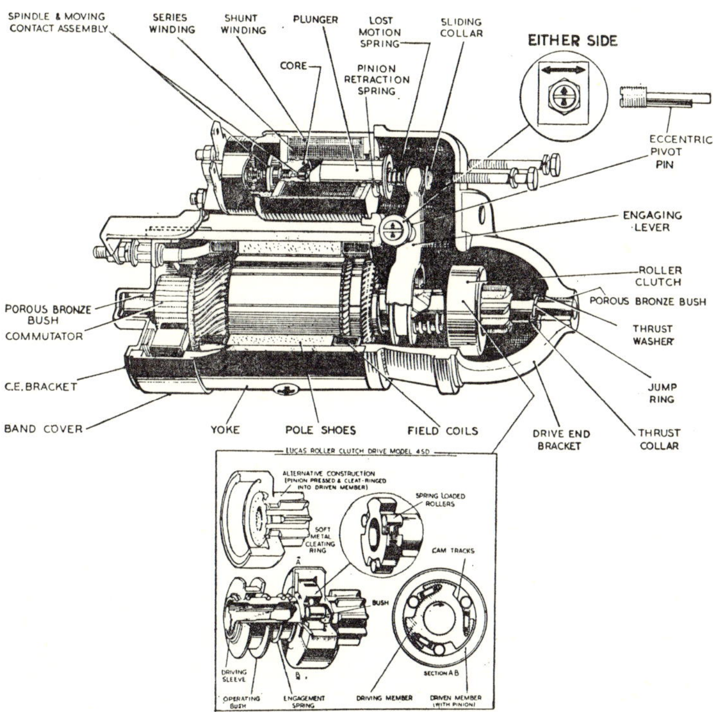

Lucas M 35 G pre-engaged starter, as used on the larger-capacity Vauxhall engines.

For example, the radiator in the HB is of tube-and-centre construction, giving low restriction to air and coolant flow. Higher coolant pressures are possible, so the cap was designed to hold a pressure of 13 psi, compared with the HA cap's maximum of 7 psi. The water pump, with fan and thermostat incorporated as a unit, was mounted on the cylinder head only, thus eliminating the need for a back-plate. Fan diameter was reduced to decrease vibration, with four blades instead of two. The entire exhaust system was redesigned, with two silencers 10-in. long, the leading silencer having a double skin to reduce drumming. The system was now mounted to the longitudinal members, not direct to the under-body, and for the "90" engine the exhaust system incorporated twin leading pipes.

The gearbox was basically the same as that which received praise on the HA-series, but, again, there were detail changes for performance improvement—and nobody could have seen these simply from a Motor Show catalogue. The rear cover and mainshaft were made longer and the propeller shaft correspondingly shorter. This saves weight, gives a smoother power take-up, and improves the life of all the drive-line components. In addition, the propeller shaft was given improved dynamic balancing.

Nevertheless, the gear-shift remained basically the same as on the HA-series, because Vauxhall owners liked it that way; so anyone simply peering into the driving position of an HB for the first time would fail to realise what changes had, in fact been made in the transmission.

Similarly, the 8 by $1\frac{1}{4}$-in. drum brakes on the HB were kept much the same as on the HA, but the optional disc front brakes were given larger calipers. The friction-pad area was also increased. Further, the handbrake was given a very simple run, through a minimum of guide-points to the rear brakes.

One cannot see some design changes simply by static inspection of a car. For instance, one of the most significant changes compared with the suspension on the HA-series Viva was the revised position of the 'roll-axis', which is the axis about which the body rolls. By raising this longitudinal axis by 4·75 in., the distance between the spring centre of gravity of the Viva and the roll axis is reduced. This gave a roll moment (the force which makes a car roll) 25 per cent lower than on the HA-series. In simple terms, this meant that a driver cornering at a gentle speed would experience 33 per cent less roll than on the original Viva, and about 10 per cent less roll at high, rally-type cornering speeds. Additionally, there were important—but unseen—changes in the steering and in other mechanical features of the HB-series. This example applies only to Viva HA/HB modifications, but there are similar improvements continuously being introduced after rigorous testing.

With Vauxhall's Chaul End research laboratory, the testing procedures at Luton and Ellesmere Port, and the 700-acre Millbrook proving ground, a key to Vauxhall's success is obviously this continual research and testing for even further refinements and reliability.

Chief Engineer John Alden puts it like this: 'The entire philosophy of present-day test methods is revealed in this process of ever-increasing and steadily-refined testing at all stages of development, and of repeating and adding tests throughout the entire life of the model. This permits the introduction of further refinement and improvement during the production run of a model so that maximum customer-satisfaction can be obtained.

'It also gives increasing knowledge of materials and techniques for the next design project to be undertaken—a continuous and self-analytical programme that results in better cars and commercial vehicles for more people.'

Index